KENTUCKY
REAL ESTATE LICENSE LAW HANDBOOK

Third Edition

COPYRIGHT© 2018
Virginia L. Lawson Seminars, Inc.

For permission to use material from this text, contact us by
telephone at (859) 396-1616
e-mail: ginnylawson@virginialawsonseminars.org
website: http://www.virginialawsonseminars.org
mail: 3306 Clays Mill Road, Suite 207
Lexington, Kentucky 40503

Printed in United States of America
18, 19, 20, 21, 22

ISBN: 978-0-9905837-4-5

Preface

This is the third edition of Kentucky Real Estate License Law Handbook. License law, like all real estate law, seems to be changing on a daily basis. As a former REALTOR®, I know how challenging the business can be and how fast it changes. Although I've been an attorney since 1984, limiting my practice to real estate law, this book is not designed to give legal advice. It is for educational purposes only and all who read it should consult their personal attorney before taking any action based upon anything they read in this book. I am not speaking for the Kentucky Real Estate Commission, for the Kentucky Association of REALTORS®, or for any of the local boards and associations. The opinions expressed herein are mine and mine only from over 32 years of experience representing licensees in courts, before the Kentucky Real Estate Commission and other administrative agencies, attending KREC monthly meetings, trade association meetings and conventions, and in discussions with other professionals in the industry.

In 2004 I wrote *Kentucky Real Estate Law*, published by Thomson South-Western. Some of you may have that book. If so, this book is an update of Chapters 5, 6, 7, 8, and 9. Because these books contain law, they are outdated quickly. I cannot believe it has been over ten (10) years since my first book. This is the second edition of Kentucky Real Estate License Law Handbook. Since then, there have been many changes in the licensing laws and regulations and in the interpretations of those laws and regulations some of these changes occurred in the past few months. My goal here is to update you on all of those changes. What I cannot guarantee is that more changes will not be made in the upcoming months. Always check with your personal attorney for specific situations and for personal legal advice.

INFORMATION CONTAINED IN THIS BOOK IS CURRENT THROUGH JULY 19, 2017. CONSULT THE KREC WEBSITE OR LICENSE LAW MANUAL FOR CHANGES AFTER THAT DATE.

Acknowledgement

Over the years I've made many good friends in the real estate industry. They've been supportive of my practice of law and teaching. I hope this book will be of help to them. One friend, Sandye Hackney, an Associate Professor of Real Estate at Bluegrass Community and Technical College, had to keep asking for the second edition of the book, and will be, hopefully, pleasantly surprised, that the third edition was published before she needed to ask! I also appreciate the assistance of my instructor friends, Joyce Sterling and Todd Thornton, who have sent me notes about awkward sentences and typos in the first two editions, and Donna Miller, who e-mails me some very interesting questions from her classes that make me think about material in the book. I appreciate the support of Tom Lambuth, owner of Career Development Center, for his encouragement in my teaching and writing endeavors. To all of the instructors who use my book in their classes, I say big thanks!

Thanks also to Kelly Alexander, a dear friend and attorney, who double-checked the legal citations and proofed legal language as I've been writing these books. And, thanks to Fred Rodgers, Attorney Associate in our firm, for helping me work through formatting issues with the software program and for preparing the index.

Thanks to my office team for their help keeping the office going while I've been out of the office writing -- Attorneys Vince Eiden and Fred Rodgers; Office Manager, Lisa Horne; Paralegal Jaime Ballard; and Legal Assistant Lisa Gooch.

A big thanks to my husband, Dr. George P. Weick, who is my editor and technical expert (technology and I are often at odds!), and to my toy poodle, Joyanna, who waits patiently for me to come upstairs after I finish working and hold her. Since writing the first edition I lost my wonderful tiny toy poodle, Brinkley, in a terrible accident, and since writing the second edition I lost my sweet toy poodle, Shellie, to cancer. I miss them both and think of them often.

I am always thankful for the memory of my supportive parents, James A. and Nettie M. Lawson. They encouraged me and always said the key to success is a good education, hard work, and solid reputation. I appreciate their advice and miss them dearly.

About the Author

Virginia "Ginny" L. Lawson, a Lexington, Kentucky, native has been practicing law throughout the Commonwealth of Kentucky law since 1984. She holds Martindale-

Hubbell AV Preeminent® rating (the highest peer rating standard signifying that the lawyer's reviewed peers rank her at the highest level of professional excellence for her legal knowledge, communication skills and ethical standards). *The National Law Journal* has recognized her as one of the nation's Top Rated Lawyers. She is a member of the American Bar Association, Kentucky Bar Association, and Fayette County Bar Association. She is admitted to practice both in federal and state courts.

Although her personal practice is limited to real estate, business, and estate/probate law, her firm, Virginia L. Lawson & Associates, P.S.C., also handles cases in other areas of law. Her real estate practice includes real estate litigation, contract formation and negotiations, closings, foreclosures, and brokerage representation. She counts many individuals, sole proprietorships, limited liability companies and corporations as her clients. Families use her services to help with planning their estates and probating their family wills.

Virginia graduated from Lafayette High School, Lexington Technical Institute with a degree in Management Technology, Eastern Kentucky University with a Bachelor of Business Administration in Real Estate, and the Brandeis School of Law at the University of Louisville. After finishing her undergraduate business degree with a major in real estate at Eastern Kentucky University, she worked as a REALTOR® for seven years prior to practicing law.

Ginny has been active in the real estate industry in a variety of capacities, including representing numerous boards and associations of REALTORS®, real estate brokers, and mortgage lenders. A large part of her practice includes litigation defense for providers of professional liability insurance for real estate licensees. These cases have been before the Kentucky Real Estate Commission, the Kentucky Auctioneers Board, the Kentucky Real Estate Appraisers Board, Professional Standards Committees, District Courts, Circuit Courts, the Kentucky Court of Appeals, and the Kentucky Supreme Court.

As a member of the first Kentucky Bar Association Committee on Alternate Dispute Resolution, she is active throughout Kentucky as a mediator in real estate cases. She has extensive experience in consulting with other attorneys in real estate cases.

She has taught numerous real estate law classes for universities, colleges, proprietary schools, real estate foundations, state licensing agencies, and brokerages. Ginny developed and taught for a number of years pre-license classes for Eastern Kentucky University. In addition to teaching, she is the author of eight books: *Kentucky Real Estate License Law Handbook, first, second, and third editions; Don't Let Wills, Estates and Trusts be the Death of You; Kentucky Real Estate Law; Sales Contracts for the Real Estate Professional; AMP Real Estate Exam Preparation; Kentucky Real Estate License Law Tutorial;* and *Law of Agency.* She writes articles appearing in newsletters, trade publications, newspapers, and journals about legal aspects of real estate, including agency, anti-trust, fair housing, disclosure, risk reduction, and contracts.

Brief Table of Contents

If you have a copy of my *Kentucky Real Estate Law* book, Chapter 1 of this book updates Chapter 5, Chapter 2 updates Chapter 6, Chapter 3 updates Chapter 7, Chapter 4 updates Chapter 8, and Chapter 5 updates Chapter 9. The remaining chapters in *Kentucky Real Estate Law* have not changed, except for changes to Chapter 14 relating to the HUD-1 Settlement Statement.

Table of Contents

CHAPTER 1

BROKERS AND SALES ASSOCIATES
Licensing Requirements, REALTORS®, Continuing Education, Post-Licensing Education, Errors & Omissions Insurance

Statutes and Administration Regulations

Chapter Objectives

This chapter reviews the licensing statutes and regulations that govern real estate brokers and sales associates. Specific licensing and continuing education requirements are included. The section on REALTORS® explains the difference between real estate agents and REALTORS®. In the last section, the reader will learn about the errors and omissions insurance that all licensees must carry. Frequently asked questions that will be answered in Chapter 1 are:

1. What is a real estate broker?
2. Is there a difference between a broker and a principal broker?
3. Are all real estate agents REALTORS®?
4. Does everyone dealing in real estate for third parties need a license or are there exceptions to licensing?
5. How much education is required to obtain a real estate license?
6. Other than education, what else is required to get a license?
7. Is a criminal records background check required for licensees?
8. If you are licensed in another state, what are the requirements to get a Kentucky license?
9. How often must real estate licenses be renewed?
10. What are the continuing education requirements for real estate brokers and sales associates?
11. What is post-licensing education and who is required to take it?
12. What happens if a licensee does not complete required continuing education and post-licensing classes?
13. May a licensee have an unlicensed personal assistant?
14. Are brokers and sales associates required to have professional liability insurance?
15. Can the KREC monitor approved real estate instructors in the classroom?

Key Terms

A review of the key terms prior to reading this chapter will assist you in understanding the license law relating to material in the chapter. It is always important to know how a certain word, term, or phrase is used in the particular statute or regulation you are studying. You will learn that sometimes a word, term, or phrase means something different from statute to statute. Each word is highlighted in the text the first time it appears in the book. There is a comprehensive Glossary in the back of the book.

Accredited Institution	Adequate Supervision
Affiliation Fee	Approved Classes
Approved Instructor	Approved Real Estate School
Branch Office	Broker
Broker-affiliated training program	Broker Core Class
Broker Management Skills Class	Commercial Real Estate Brokerage
Consent to Service	Continuing Education
Continuing Education Providers	Criminal Records Background Check
Delinquency Plan	Designated Manager
Errors and Omissions Insurance	Independent Contractor
Kentucky Core Class	License Cancellation
License Escrow	License Recognition
License Renewal	Non-licensed Personal Assistant
Post-License Education	Power of Attorney
Principal Broker	Real Estate
Real Estate Brokerage	REALTOR®
Reciprocal Licensing	Referral Fee
Sales Associate	Unlicensed Assistant

Accredited Institution: A college or university, accredited by appropriately recognized educational associations, or chartered and licensed in Kentucky, that grants credits toward a program for either an associate, baccalaureate, graduate, or professional degree. KRS 324.010(8).

Adequate Supervision: The license law requirement for a Principal Broker to supervise his affiliates to assure they are adhering to the license law and regulations. Although the license law does not outline specific activities, it is reasonable to assume that adequate supervision includes training and educating in the practice of real estate, and assisting affiliates in their day to day activities as needed. KRS 324.160(6).

Affiliation Fee: A fee that a Principal Broker would charge a licensee to join his office. This fee is prohibited under KRS 324.288.

Approved Classes: Pre-license, post-license, and continuing education courses/classes that have been approved by the Kentucky Real Estate Commission after meeting criteria set out in 201 KAR 11:170 and 201 KAR 11:235   Without this approval, real estate classes cannot be used to satisfy pre-license, post-license, or continuing education credit.

Approved Instructor: Teachers who have met the requirements of 201 KAR 11:175 to teach real estate classes/courses for pre-license, post-license, and continuing education credit.

Approved Real Estate School: A school that has a certificate of approval from the Kentucky Commission of Proprietary Education, or other regulatory bodies that exercise jurisdiction over accreditation and approval, and the Kentucky Real Estate Commission. The school must also be in good standing with these entities. KRS 324.010(7). Approved schools are also referred to as a continuing education provider. KRS 201 KAR 11:232 outlines in detail the criteria for all activities of the continuing education provider.

Branch Office: Term used to indicate an office operated by the Principal Broker that is not the main brokerage office.   KRS 324.112 outlines the license law requirements necessary to maintain a branch office.

Broker: A person who holds a broker's license issued pursuant to KRS 324.046. A broker may or may not also be the Principal Broker of the real estate company that holds her license.

Broker-affiliated training program: One or more post-license educational courses offered for post-licensed education credit provided or sponsored by a real estate principal broker.

Broker Core Class: In recent years, the Kentucky Real Estate Commission created a new core class that was open only to licensees with a broker's license. The class was titled "Risk Management for Brokers." This class could be taken by qualified licensees instead of the Kentucky Core class. Material in the class is more advanced and in greater detail than the material in the Kentucky Core class. In December 2015, after the course material was revised, the Commissioners voted to allow not only licensees with a broker's license to take the class, but also associates who are designated managers, office managers, team leaders, and any other licensee in a management position. Each attendee with an associate's license must submit an affidavit, satisfactory to the KREC, stating that she is, in fact, in a management position.

Broker Management Class a/k/a Broker Management Skills Class: This is a class approved by the KREC that all applicants for the broker's license must take and complete prior to taking the broker's licensing examination. Providers submit outlines and course materials for the KREC approval. 201 KAR 11:450.

Commercial Real Estate Brokerage: As used in KRS 324.235 - KRS 324.238, any parcel of real estate located in this state that is lawfully used for sales, retail, wholesale, office, research, institutional, warehouse, manufacturing, or industrial purposes; lawfully used primarily for multi-family residential purposes involving five (5) or more dwelling units; or zoned for a business or commercial use by a planning unit pursuant to KRS Chapter 100.

Consent to Service: Out-of-state principal brokers sign a "consent to service of jurisdiction" document agreeing that they may be sued in Kentucky. Otherwise, a consumer wanting to file a lawsuit against the principal broker would be required to file the lawsuit in the state where the principal broker does business and/or resides (depending on that state's laws). Filing a lawsuit outside of Kentucky against a principal broker for negligence in Kentucky would create a hardship on the consumer. Signing this form is one of the KREC requirements for allowing an out-of-state principal broker to do business in Kentucky.

Continuing Education: Education relating to the practice of real estate and real estate law that must be taken annually by licensees, unless they were licensed prior to June 19, 1976, or after January 1, 2016. Licensees licensed before June 19, 1976 are not required to take Continuing Education classes. And, licensees licensed after January 1, 2016 do not have to take continuing education for the first two years of licensure, because they are taking post-license classes. After the two-year post licensing classes, these licenses are on the regular continuing education schedule. The KREC must approve the course content and instructors. KRS 324.085 and 201 KAR 11:230.

Continuing Education Providers: Effective December 4, 2015, 201 KAR 11:230, was created to address all continuing education provider requirements for classes and related issues. Approved Real Estate Schools that offer continuing education classes are also referred to as Continuing Education Providers.

Criminal Records Background Check: Applicants for a license must obtain a criminal records check from the FBI or from any other commission-approved criminal background-checking provider or company furnishing identification records that are comparable to those provided by the FBI, as determined by the commission. At this time, the applicant may use the Kentucky State Police Process to request their FBI report. The background check must be ordered prior to taking the examination. 201 KAR 11:430.

Delinquency Plan: A licensee who does not complete his continuing education classes by December 31st may enter into a plan with the KREC to complete the classes. 201 KAR 11:230, Section 6.

Designated Manager: A licensed sales associate or broker who manages a main or branch office for the principal broker, at the principal broker's direction, and has managing authority over the activities of the sales associates at that office. KRS 324.010(11).

Errors and Omissions Insurance: Professional liability insurance (commonly referred to as E&O Insurance) that must be carried by all active licensees. KRS 324.395. Licensees whose licenses are in escrow are not required to carry E&O Insurance. KRS 324.310(2).

Independent Contractor: A self-employed individual. Most real estate licensees work as independent contractors.

Kentucky Core Class: A continuing education class developed by the KREC that all licensees are required to take once every four years. The KREC has also developed a Core class for licensees with broker's licenses and associates in management positions which was recently been renamed "Broker Core." Those with broker's licenses and associates with management positions have a choice of which Core they want to take. The Broker Core is a more advanced class. 201 KAR 11:230(2).

License cancellation: This term is used when the KREC withdraws a licensee's authority to sell real estate because the agent failed to renew a license, wrote the KREC a check for fees that is not honored, failed to re-affiliate with a principal broker, or failed to complete requirements for continuing or post-license education. Cancellation may also occur if the licensee failed to notify the commission of a change in the broker's business location, a change in the brokerage firm name, the sales associate's transfer from one broker to another one, change of residence address within ten (10) days, and/or a change of surname. A licensee's failure to re-affiliate with another principal broker once her license is returned to the KREC by her current broker will result in cancellation. KRS 324.010(16); KRS 324.330(1)(2); 201 KAR 11:225, Section 1; 201 KAR 11:147(2)(b).

License Escrow: This is an inactive status for licensees. A licensee must request his license be placed in escrow and cannot rely on his principal broker to place the license in escrow. While the license is in escrow the licensee may not engage in any brokerage activity. KRS 324.310.

License Recognition: Process for out-of-state licensees to receive a Kentucky license. This is the process that replaced reciprocal licensing. 201 KAR 11:215.

License Renewal: All licenses (active and in escrow) must be renewed annually. Licenses are active from April 1st to March 31st. 201 KAR 11:225.

Non-licensed personal assistant: The license law provides for unlicensed people to perform certain tasks related to real estate brokerage under the supervision of a licensee. These people are also referred to as unlicensed assistants. KRS 324.030(6); 201 KAR 11:440.

Post-License Education: A licensee who is issued an initial sales associate license after January 1, 2016, shall complete forty-eight (48) classroom or online hours of commission-approved post-license education. KRS 324.085(2).

Power of Attorney: A written document signed by the principal authorizing the agent, known as the attorney-in-fact, to act on behalf of the principal.

Principal Broker: The person that is responsible for the operation of the brokerage and for the adequate supervision of all licensees affiliated with the brokerage. KRS 324.010(4).

Case: Attorney Attempted to use Attorney Exception and the Exception Did Not Apply

Kentucky Bar Ass'n v. Burbank, Ky., 539 S.W.2d 312 (1976)

William B. Burbank, who was an attorney licensed by the Kentucky Bar Association, was practicing law in Louisville, KY. He did not have a real estate license. In February and March of 1975, he represented Virginia Collins, his girlfriend, in her negotiations to purchase real estate that was listed with the Paul Semonin Company, a local real estate firm. In conversations with the real estate agents, he informed them that if his client purchased a particular piece of property in which he had participated in the negotiations, the commission must be split with him.

The Kentucky Bar Association felt that it was unethical for Burbank to split a commission with a real estate agency when he was not a licensed real estate agent. It felt that he had violated the standards of conduct outlined in the Code of Professional Responsibility. There was also concern that he was representing one client, the buyer, while asking a non-client, the seller, to pay his fee.

Mr. Burbank's defense was that he did not want the commission for himself, but that he was trying to save money for the buyer. He also defended by saying he believed his license to practice law also gave him the right to practice real estate.

On review of the case, the Supreme Court felt that his "conduct in requesting a split in the fee was unethical, and was of the type calculated to bring the profession into disrepute." At page 313 of its opinion the Justices stated:

> "The practice of law is an honorable profession. No lawyer should ever do any act or acts that would in any way reflect upon the honorable profession of law. Every lawyer worthy of the profession should, like 'Caesars's Wife' be above suspicion….Because of his position in society, even minor violations of the law by a lawyer may tend to lessen public confidence in the legal profession. Obedience to law exemplifies respect for law. To lawyers especially, respect for the law should be more than a platitude."

The Supreme Court upheld the Kentucky Bar Association Board of Governors recommendation that Mr. Burbank be publicly reprimanded and ordered to pay the costs of the action.

Anyone acting under a court order may handle **real estate** transactions without having either a broker's or sales associate's license. KRS 324.030(4). Executors who are settling estates, trustees in bankruptcy proceedings, receivers in business dissolutions, and trustees acting under a trust agreement, deed of trust, or will are all examples of people who may be appointed by the court to purchase, sell, or lease real property. In addition to the appointees acting without a license, their regular salaried employees who are employed to assist in these transactions are also exempt. These people cannot be compensated for their services by receiving a commission.

KRS 324.980 exempts a person from being licensed who is "engaged solely in the business of compiling and categorizing information concerning the location and availability of real property . . . who furnished information to prospective tenants for a fee." This exemption does not permit the person to market and show the property.

The license law permits unlicensed people to perform services for the licensee that brings the **unlicensed assistant** in direct contact with consumers. A requirement of this law is that the unlicensed person must be working under the direct supervision of a licensed real estate broker or the supervising licensee appointed by the principal broker. In the license law this person is referred to as a non-licensed personal assistant. 201 KAR 11:440. See Chapter 3 for further discussion of unlicensed assistants/non-licensed personal assistants.

Licensing Exception for Commercial Real Estate Brokerage

KRS 324.235 through KRS 324.238 provide for out-of-state licensees to practice **commercial real estate brokerage** in Kentucky under a very narrowly defined exception. Because of a lawsuit filed against the Kentucky Real Estate Commission by a large out-of-state real estate brokerage a few years ago, this exception was created. The brokerage filed the lawsuit under the Commerce Clause of the United States Constitution. Basically, in very general terms, this clause requires states to cooperate with each other in the furtherance of commerce. At that time, Kentucky was referred to as a "turf state." That is, unless you had a license in Kentucky you could not broker real estate located in Kentucky under any circumstances. Allegations were that the "turf state" policy did not further commerce. Brokers with licenses in different states wanted to broker real estate without obtaining a Kentucky license.

These statutes are very specific in their requirements. The basic provision is that the out-of-state broker must enter into a written cooperation agreement with a Kentucky principal broker. Some of the other requirements are that the agreement must reference the commercial transactions that will be brokered, all escrow funds, security deposits, and other money relating to the transaction must be held in Kentucky, and all advertising must include the Kentucky cooperating broker. An irrevocable consent that all legal actions may be brought in Kentucky must be signed by the out-of-state broker, and a criminal background check must be provided from the out-of-state broker and the out-of-state licensee actually working in Kentucky.

Because of the extreme detail in these statutes, the Kentucky principal broker agreeing to cooperate with the out-of-state broker should review them carefully when entering into an agreement. It is important for the Kentucky principal broker to remember that the out-of-state broker is required to work under the direct supervision and control of the Kentucky cooperating broker.

Principal Broker

Owners of brokerages do not have to have a real estate license, but each brokerage must have a principal broker that is responsible for all licensees affiliated with the office. As defined by the licensing statute, KRS 324.010(4), a principal broker is "a person licensed as a broker under KRS 324.046 who, in addition to performing acts of real estate brokerage or transactions comprehended by that definition, is the single broker responsible for the operation of the company with which he or she is associated." A special license is not required to be a principal broker, but the Kentucky Real Estate Commission must be notified that a licensed broker is becoming the principal broker for the company.

The principal broker must exercise **adequate supervision** over the licensees affiliated with the office to ensure that all of the licensees and all of the company employees follow the licensing laws and regulations. To assist in these supervisory duties, the principal broker may designate a manager who must also have a broker's license. If the principal broker and/or the **designated manager** fail to adequately supervise the licensees and employees, the principal broker and/or his designated manager may be disciplined by the Kentucky Real Estate Commission for violating the licensing statute. KRS 324.160(6).

Although the amount of supervision may vary from company to company, depending on the knowledge and experience of the agents, it is clear that the supervision must be adequate enough to protect the consumer dealing with the affiliated licensees and company employees. Principal brokers, or their designated managers, must insure that the agents affiliated with the company have enough education and training to do the work for which they are licensed. Because the real estate business has had many changes recently, adequate supervision would include insuring that educational opportunities are available for the licensees. The principal broker, or designated manager, should be available to answer agent's questions on a daily basis. And, the principal broker, or designated manager, should have enough knowledge and understanding of the transactions occurring in the office to prevent an agent from violating the license law, either accidentally or intentionally.

The licensing statute also provides that the principal broker may be held primarily liable for acts of agents affiliated with the company if he had knowledge that the law was being violated and failed to prevent it. Primary liability means the principal broker would be liable for the violation of the statute, although he did not actually commit the act that broke the law. For example, in a case where the agent misrepresented the condition of a roof and the broker knew the agent was making a misrepresentation and failed to stop the agent, the broker would be liable for both the misstatement made about the roof, as well as for the failure to adequately supervise the licensee. KRS 324.160(6).

To assist the principal broker in her duties, she may appoint a **designated manager**. Principal brokers have frequently had office managers that assisted in the day-to-day operation of the business, but that person did not have recognition under the license law. KRS 324.010(11) created a new definition for this person. The designated manager may be either a sales associate or broker who manages a main or **branch office** for the principal broker, at the principal broker's direction, and has managing authority over the activities of the sales associates at that office. And, as a consequence of the designation, she is responsible under the license law for adequate supervision, along with the principal broker.

When a broker or sales associate places his license with a principal broker, this is referred to as "**affiliation**." Under the license law, KRS 324.010(15), affiliation is defined as: "the relationship agreed upon between a licensee and a principal broker and reported to the commission, where the licensee places his license with the principal broker for supervision of the licensee's real estate brokerage activity." Principal brokers may not charge licensees an **affiliation fee**. An "affiliation fee" is defined in the license law as "any fee or compensation paid by a licensee, to any person, for the privilege of listing his license with a particular principal broker, in records submitted to the commission." KRS 324.288. Upon request of the licensee the principal broker must return the affiliate's license to the KREC or he is in violation of the statute. KRS 324.312. Although "affiliate" is used in the license law, most people in the real estate industry refer to the licensees affiliated with the principal broker as "associates" instead of "affiliates." Either is acceptable.

Principal brokers who are residents of Kentucky must maintain an actual place of business in the state. This requirement is not met until the principal broker has an actual street address. Having just a post office box does not enable the broker to comply with the law. KRS 324.115(1).

Nonresident principal brokers are not required to have an actual place of business in the state if they have a place of business in the state where they were originally licensed, if that state does not require the principal broker to have a business location in Kentucky, and if the reciprocity agreement between that state and Kentucky is not violated. KRS 324.115(2). Kentucky no longer has reciprocity agreements, but this language remains in the statute. Instead of reciprocity, Kentucky has **"license recognition"** which will be discussed later in this chapter.

Branch offices may be maintained by principal brokers; however, a **branch office** farther than 100 miles from the main office must have a branch office manager with a broker's license. A sales associate may manage a branch office inside a 100 mile radius of the main office if he has an associate's license, plus two years experience in the real estate business, averaging at least twenty hours per week for a period of 24 months prior.

The principal broker must register the branch office with the KREC within 10 days of the creation of the branch office. KRS 324.112(1)(2)(3).

KRS 324.112(4) requires that the actual licenses of the agents associated with a principal broker be kept at the office location where the licensee works. Under prior law, the licenses had to be on display, but under current law the licenses may be kept in a file. The licenses should be available for inspection by anyone coming into the office to verify that a person is actually licensed.

With one exception, a real estate brokerage may have only one principal broker. That exception occurs when a principal broker wants to close her office and needs to have an office to work from until all of her pending business is finalized. The criteria that must be met for the principal broker to affiliate with the other principal broker are: the principal broker closing her office cannot have any other licensee affiliated with her; both principal brokers must inform the Kentucky Real Estate Commission that the purpose of their affiliation is to close one office; and both principal brokers assure the Commission that their affiliation and that closing the one office will not adversely affect consumers. KRS 324.112(5).

Independent Contractors Affiliated licensees may be employees; however, most are not employees and work as **independent contractors**. As independent contractors, the licensees are self-employed and self-directed. The principal broker retains the licensees to perform real estate services for consumers on behalf of the brokerage, but the principal broker cannot control how and when they perform those services.

The principal broker can set office policies and procedures for the company and can require the licensees to perform their work in a legal, professional, ethical, and honest manner. However, he cannot tell them when to come to work, when to leave work, and how to practice real estate. If the principal broker wants to maintain the independent contractor status of his affiliates, he must not exercise too much control over their day to day activities. Requiring licensees to attend meetings, have regular office hours, and perform certain tasks for the company may change the character of the relationship from independent contractor to employee.

If the associate is an independent contractors, the commissions they earn are paid to them by the principal broker without federal, state, and local income taxes being deducted, and without social security taxes being withheld. The licensee is responsible for paying his own income and social security taxes. Because social security taxes are not withheld, the company does not have to match the social security paid by the licensees. Therefore, the full amount of the social security taxes is paid by the independent contractor.

The independent contractor status is one that is watched closely by the Internal Revenue Service. If the IRS determines that an employer/employee relationship exists instead of an independent contractor relationship, the principal broker may be liable for all back taxes not withheld and all social security matching funds. Some practices that may trigger the employer/employee relationship include the broker's paying licensee fees and board membership dues for the licensees; requiring attendance at weekly or monthly sales meetings; requiring the licensees to answer the phone in the office at set times; or reimbursing licensee expenses for entertainment of clients or for automobile usage.

Another important consideration is liability. An employer/employee relationship makes the employer legally liable for negligent acts of the employee. Although the principal broker must adequately supervise the licensee under the licensing laws, the extent of liability for negligent acts is less with an independent contractor than with an employee. A principal broker may only be held to be primarily liable for negligence if he knew of the negligence and failed to stop it.

Termination of Affiliation

The relationship between the principal broker and affiliated licensees is typically considered to be a relationship at will. If the broker wants the licensee to leave her office, she has a right to terminate the relationship without cause. A licensee who chooses to change brokerages may do so without giving the broker a reason or notice.

When the principal broker terminates the relationship with the licensee, or when the licensee requests his license be returned to the KREC, the principal broker must release the licensee. In the past, the broker had to deliver or mail the license to the Commission. Now the KREC has a process for making certain changes on-line, including releasing a licensee. The details may be found at www.krec.ky.gov. Either process may be used; however, the on-line method is preferred.

A relatively recent change to the license law seems to define "immediate" as five (5) business days. Should the principal broker fail to release the license within the five (5) business days after being requested to do so, he will be in violation of KRS 324.160(4)(u) and KRS 324.312(2). A violation of this subsection would "constitute improper, fraudulent, or dishonest dealing" by the principal broker. KRS 324.160(4)(u).

Another change in the license law allows the principal broker to have a representative in the brokerage stamp the principal broker's name on the license if the principal broker is out of town. Should the principal broker be unable to find the license, he can send a letter to the KREC releasing the licensee with a statement that the license has been lost. At the time the license is released, the principal broker must send the licensee a letter to his last known address informing him that his license has been returned. A copy of the letter to the licensee must be sent to the Commission along with the license. KRS 324.310(1). A licensee cannot perform real estate services, after the license has been returned to the KREC, until a new license with a new principal broker has been issued. KRS 324.310(2) and (3).

Author's note: A prudent principal broker would never have her signature on a rubber stamp. That seems to be taking an absolutely unnecessary risk.

Requirements to Obtain a License

The statutes and regulations set forth the specific requirements for a person to obtain a broker or sales associate's license, and also set forth the requirements to maintain the license. One of the duties of the Kentucky Real Estate Commission is to either conduct license examinations or contract with a company to conduct the examinations. Currently, the Commission contracts with PSI Services, LLC (also referred to as PSI), a national testing company, to administer the examinations. Because the testing service changes on occasion, anyone seeking a license should go to the KREC website to determine the current licensing company. To assure that the test questions conform to Kentucky law and practice, the Commission has a group of subject matter experts that reviews the test questions.

Qualifications for Obtaining a License

Licenses shall be granted only to people who are trustworthy and competent. They are required to transact their business as brokers and sales associates in a manner that safeguards the interest of the public. The Kentucky Real Estate Commission will only grant licenses to people who satisfactorily prove through their application and testing that they meet these requirements. "Examinations shall be of the scope and wording sufficient in the judgment of the commission to establish the competency of the applicant to act as a broker or sales associate." KRS 324.045(1), (2). Applicants for initial licensure must be at least 18 years old. KRS 324.040(3).

Sales associates wanting to become brokers must have had a sales associate's license and been actively engaged in the real estate business for a period of two years. During the two year period, the applicant must have worked an average of 20 hours per week. The broker or brokers with whom the sales associate has been affiliated must sign a notarized affidavit that this requirement has been met. KRS 324.046(1)(b).

An exception to the two year experience is made when the applicant has an associate degree (2 year degree) or a baccalaureate degree (4 year degree) with a major or minor in real estate. The Commission may reduce the two year experience requirement to one year if the applicant has an associate degree or baccalaureate degree with a major or minor in real estate. KRS 324.046(4).

Applications for both the sales associate's and broker's license must be on forms prepared and furnished by the Commission. Every applicant must state whether or not he has ever had a license suspended or revoked, must include the name of the person or company that he will be affiliated with, along with the location of the company, must state his business and residence address, and must state how long he has been in the real estate business (if he has previously had a license). KRS 324.040.

When the applicant signs the application, he is signing a sworn statement that the information is true and correct. In the event the information is not true and correct, the license application may be denied if the false information is discovered before the license is issued, or the license may be suspended or revoked if the false information is discovered after the license is issued. KRS 324.160(a).

The licensing regulations provides for penalties if an applicant or licensee misrepresent facts on a sworn statement. In addition to the civil penalties outlined in KRS 324.160, the KREC can now seek a criminal indictment for perjury. Clearly, the Commission wants licensees to understand the importance of signing sworn statements that are absolutely true.

Educational Requirements Applicants for a real estate license must meet certain educational requirements before taking the licensing examination. The minimum education requirement for licensure is a high school diploma or its equivalent. KRS 324.040(3). A copy of the high school or G.E.D. diploma must be submitted as proof of education.

In lieu of proof of high school graduation or a GED, the applicant may submit an official transcript from a United States institution, or from an institution outside the United States, which indicates successful post-secondary completion of a degree program, or 28 academic semester hours or the equivalent. 201 KAR 11:210, Section 1.

The applicant shall provide a letter to the KREC indicating that the curriculum of the proffered education is equivalent to a high diploma or GED. The comparison shall be made by an education credential service provider with membership in the National Association of Credential Evaluation Services. 201 KAR 11:210, Section 2(1)(2).

Licensees shall apply for a license within 60 days after passing the examination. Failure to apply within said period shall require the applicant be re-examined. 201 KAR 11:210, Section 2(3).

In addition to having a high school diploma or its equivalent, the applicant must also complete classes in real estate. The sales associate applicant, prior to taking the licensing examination, must have completed at least six (6) academic credit hours at an **accredited institution** (college or university) in real estate classes or 96 classroom hours from a Kentucky **approved real estate school**. KRS 324.046(2). The six credit hours for colleges and universities is usually completed by taking two three-hour classes that continue for a full semester. Approved real estate schools have different schedules that may enable the student to complete the classroom hour requirement in as little as two weeks.

An accredited college or university is one that grants credits towards an associate degree, a baccalaureate degree, graduate or professional degree and that is accredited by "an appropriately recognized educational association chartered and licensed in Kentucky." KRS 324.010(8). An approved real estate school is either one of two types. One is a school that has been given a certificate of approval by the State Board of Proprietary Education or other appropriate regulatory body, and that also been approved by the Kentucky Real Estate Commission. This school must also be in good standing with its regulatory agency. The second type is a program that has been recognized by the National Association of REALTORS, that has been reviewed by the Kentucky Real Estate Commission, and that has been deemed an approved real estate school by the Commission. KRS 324.010(7).

For a college or university, one academic credit hour is defined as one college semester hour, and for an approved real estate school one academic credit hour consists of 16 classes that are 50 minutes long. Because college and university semesters are typically 16 weeks long, the actual time the student spends in class is the same whether they attend a college, university, or approved real estate school. 201 KAR 11:011(1).

Because there is no specific class required, the applicant may take, at her discretion, any "real estate" classes. This means the classes must be designated as real estate classes, and the focus of the material must be real estate. An applicant may choose to take principles to get an overview or may choose to take specific classes such as finance, marketing, appraising, or construction. Classes offered by approved real estate schools are geared for the student preparing to take the licensing examinations. Because of this focus, the classes comprising the 96 hours cover all of the topics found on the licensing examination. Applicants cannot use classes that were taken for **continuing education**, examination preparation or review, or competency testing to meet their real estate class education requirement.

The licensing regulations make it clear that the education director of the Kentucky Real Estate Commission reviews all courses submitted for approval, and recommends to the commission whether or not to accept a particular class. 201 KAR 11:170 outlines in detail the proposed course materials that must be submitted for review. After the Commission reviews the material, the education director shall notify the provider is the class was approved or denied for academic credit.

Broker applicants must have additional education before applying for their broker's license. KRS 324.046(1). They are required to take 21 credit hours from an accredited college or university, with at least 12 of those in real estate classes, or 336 classroom hours in real estate courses from an approved real estate school. Nine credit hours may be in any real estate topic that is chosen by the applicant. Three of the credit hours must be in a **broker management skills class**. Approved real estate schools must include 48 hours of broker management skills class in their curriculum.

The broker management skills class is not a class on real estate principles and practices; rather, it is a class on business management. Often when principal brokers have problems managing their businesses, it is not because they don't understand real estate, but because they don't understand small business management. Planning, budgeting, employee relations, and office operations are some of the topics covered in the class. One of the requirements in the broker management class is for the students to complete a sample business plan, financial plan, and office policy and procedures manual. These plans and manual must be completed within one year after completing the coursework. A

The state where the class was held approved the course for real estate continuing education credit and the course focus cannot be the real estate laws of that state. Course content must enable the licensee to better understand the real estate brokerage business and meet the content criteria prescribed by the Commission. Additionally, the class must have been taken in the calendar year for which credit is sought.

Whether or not credit will be awarded is at the discretion of the Commission. Licensees must submit their certificate of completion, and the "Out of State Continuing Education Form," (form E111 on the KREC website) to the Commission by December 31st of the calendar year for which the licensee is seeking credit. The Commission will review the information provided by the licensee to verify that the class meets the requirements of 201 KAR 11:230, Section 4 (1) through (4). If the request is denied, the KREC will notify the agent in writing with a brief explanation of the reason for the denial. 201 KAR 11:230, Section 5.

Approved Instructors

Because the KREC is concerned about the quality of education classes, there is a process followed by the Commission to approve instructors that teach pre-license, continuing education, and post-license classes. Instructor applicants must complete a Real Estate Instructor Application and submit it with a copy of a current resume, other legal documentation which may be required by the KREC, and a copy of the course outline for each class. The educational level required is either an associate, bachelor, masters, or doctorate degree from an accredited college or university in a field directly related to real estate. If the instructor applicant does not have the educational requirement, the KREC will accept five years consecutive full-time experience in the real estate area that she will be teaching. In order to meet the five year experience requirement, the applicant must have worked an average of 20 hours per week each year for the five year period. To meet the minimum requirement, the applicant may combine education, teaching, and real estate experience. A thorough familiarity of the licensing laws and the subject area taught is also required. 201 KAR 11:175, Section 1.

Approved instructors may teach pre-license classes, continuing education, and post-license classes. Unless approved by the KREC, it is a violation of the licensing law for someone, regardless of her experience and education, to teach any of these classes. 201 KAR 11:175, Section 3(2). To teach both the Kentucky Core class and the Broker Core class, approved instructors must go through an additional approval process which includes a presentation, either in the classroom or video, showing their teaching style and understanding of the material being taught.

The KREC will withdraw instructor approval for a number of reasons. Approval will be withdrawn if the instructor violates any of the licensing laws, either in his capacity as an instructor or, for instructors who also practice real estate, in his capacity as a licensee. Instructor approval shall be withdrawn if it is discovered that documentation submitted for approval is false, or if the instructor fails to provide information requested by the KREC. Approval will be withdrawn if the instructor engages in brokerage activity with a student, asks a student to participate in an investment opportunity, or recruits a student to work for a specific real estate company. 201 KAR 11:175, Section 2.

Instructors who are also licensees may receive continuing education credit for continuing education classes they teach. An instructor may receive one hour of credit for each hour taught; however, credit will not awarded more than once in a calendar year for the same course. Pre-license and post-license courses may also qualify for instructor continuing education credits.

Approved Real Estate Schools

Not only must instructors who teach pre-license classes, continuing education classes, post-licensing classes, and CORE classes be approved, the schools must also be approved by the KREC, 201 KAR 11:170. An approval shall be for a two-year period beginning November 1st. The renewal application must be submitted by October 1st of each even numbered year. A school desiring to become an approved real estate school, or one that is renewing a certification, must submit certain information to the KREC. Information required to be included with the application is (1) sample schedules and completed course outlines, (2) an instructor application; (3) a copy of the contract or agreement between the school that outlines the class schedule, grading system, and attendance requirements; (4) a copy of the written material to be used in the classroom (however, it is not necessary to submit the textbook or license law manual); (5) a sample copy of the school brochure or information promoting the school; (6) copy of legal documentation required to support an answer; and (6) a sample copy of the transcript to be used by the school. Because the approved real estate school must also be approved by the State Board for Proprietary Education, or the Kentucky Department of Education, a copy of the certification must be included in the application package.

Because license applicants must submit to a **criminal records background check**, pursuant to 201 KAR 11:170, Section 1(3), approved schools must indicate in information given the students that a criminal conviction may prevent students from obtaining a license. If the school fails to do this, its status as an approved school may be suspended until the information is changed to include the notice. Approved schools must notify the KREC within ten days of a material change in the information provided to the KREC to gain approval. A material change would be one that would affect the school's ability to be approved.

201 KAR 11:170, Section 2, sets out very specific requirements for the approved school curriculum. Those wishing to become an approved school must meet these requirements, including a closed-book monitored final examination "of at least 50 multiple choice questions for a 3 hour academic course; or 100 multiple choice questions for a 6 hour academic course" 201 KAR 11:147, Section 2(1)(d).

Additionally, approved schools may not advertise specific brokers or brokerages along with their school ads, nor can they discuss principal brokers or brokerages for the purpose of inducing or promoting affiliation with a specific principal broker or brokerage.

Permanent records of courses completed or attempted, hours completed, final grades, and Certification of Completion shall be maintained by the school for a period of three years. A copy of the Certification of Completion shall be mailed to each student. To assure compliance with these requirements, the school must permit inspection and monitoring by the KREC or by someone it designates.

Approval may be withdrawn by the KREC if information provided to obtain the initial approval or renewal is inaccurate or misleading, if the school is not in compliance with the licensing regulations, or if the instruction is deficient and the school does not correct the deficiency within 30 days. 201 KAR 11:170, Section 7. A school's approval will be immediately revoked if the school, directly or indirectly, tries to reproduce the licensing exam, either in whole or in part. 201 KAR 11:170, Section 8.

Post-License Education

Everyone receiving a license after January 1, 2016 is now required to take 48 hours of commission-approved education within two years of receiving or activating an initial sales associate's license. KRS 324.085(2). During this two-year period, the new licensee is not required to take the six hours of continuing education. 201 KAR 11:230, Section 3(3).

Post-license classes may be obtained from an accredited institution (college or university), a commission-approved real estate school or **broker-affiliated training program**, or a combination of both. A "broker-affiliated training program" means one or more post-license educational course offered for post-licensed education credit provided or sponsored by a real estate principal broker.

The 48 hours of instruction must be completed within two years, unless extended by the Commission for good cause shown. Should a license fail to complete post-license education as required, her license will be canceled.

Post-license education shall consist of 32 hours from prescribed areas of study and 16 hours from electives. The KREC has developed a three hour "Commission Licensee Compliance" course that will be three of the 32 required hours. Topics for the remaining 29 hours will include agency, contracts, financing, advertising, disclosure, fair housing, technology and data security, and risk management. Elective topics are still developing. Some of the suggested elective topics include real estate auctions, anti-trust law, appraisals and home inspection, land use, property rights, property management, real estate investment and business planning. 201 KAR 11:235, Section 4(2). Motivational and personal development classes cannot be used for elective credit. Post-license classes should be practicum-based and teach licensees practical knowledge of the business while protecting the public.

Unlike continuing education classes, a licensee may not duplicate a post-license class for credit. Licensees may not take more than nine hours of post-license education in a 24-hour period. 201 KAR 11:235, Section 4(4).

Classes may only be taught by instructors approved by the KREC following the same guidelines as pre-license and continuing education instructors. Instructors previously approved by other providers in a calendar year may submit an Education Course Application to teach the post-license classes. 201 KAR 11:235, Section 2(2).

To apply to teach a post-license class, a provider must submit a course outline broken into 15 minute increments. The outline must include course objectives, teaching methods, auxiliary aids, class materials and policies of the provider. An application signed by the sponsor indicating that the class is in compliance with law and regulations must be submitted. Along with the application, the instructor application, all advertising and brochures, and proof of school qualifications to offer post-licensing education, must be submitted. 201 KAR 11:235, Section 2(2)(a).

Providers must, at least 30 days prior to scheduling a post-license course, submit an Education Schedule (Form E-106) to the KREC. 201 KAR 11:235, Section 2(6)(a). These forms may be found on the KREC web site under Education. Each attendee should receive a certificate of completion after attending the course, and a roster of all attended must be submitted to the KREC within 10 days of conclusion of the course. 201 KAR 11:235, Section 2(6)(b). The KREC may monitor the classes unannounced. 201 KAR 11:235, Section 2(6)(d).

Like all KREC approved education classes, approval may be withdrawn for a violation of the KREC Guidelines for Classroom Management (Form E103), for falsification of attendance information submitted to the KREC, for an instructor soliciting business or selling materials to students in the classroom, for failure to provide the commission required materials, and for conducting a course not approved prior to it being offered. 201 KAR 11:235, Section 2(7).

Because this is a new statute and regulation, licensees should monitor them for possible changes and new interpretations. Always read the KREC newsletter to see updates. And, of course, read all e-mail sent to you by the KREC.

Errors and Omissions Insurance

All Kentucky licensees, except those whose licenses are in escrow, must carry professional liability insurance, commonly referred to as E&O insurance. KRS 324.395. This is a policy providing coverage for acts of professional negligence. Because it covers acts of negligence, the policy may contain certain exclusions as set forth in 201 KAR 11:220, Section 5. Among the exclusions permitted are personal injury claims; intentional fraudulent, criminal, or malicious acts by the licensee; insolvency of the licensee; securities, discrimination, and environmental cases. Because insurance carriers compete for this business, licensees should review their policies to learn exactly what is included and what is excluded. To be competitive the carriers often include coverage that they could exclude.

KRS 324.395 sets forth the requirements that licensees must have the insurance and that the Kentucky Real Estate Commission must provide for the coverage. The KREC must contract, through a competitive, sealed bid process, with an insurance company to provide group coverage at a premium not to exceed two hundred dollars ($200.00) per year. If the coverage cannot be obtained at that cost for a given year, licensees are not required to carry the insurance for that period of time.

The KREC must determine the level of coverage to be required and must establish the minimum standards for the policy. It must also determine if the policies may carry a deductible amount and if certain exemptions are permissible. KRS 324.395(5). As part of the coverage, the insurance carrier must agree not to cancel any licensee regardless of the number of claims a licensee may have had filed against him.

Licensees must be notified at least 30 days before the annual license renewal date of the coverage and of the cost for that year. KRS 324.395(6). The licensee may choose to use the state endorsed insurance company and to notify the KREC at the time of license renewal and pay the premium at that time. Or, the licensee may choose to use another insurance company instead of the KREC endorsed carrier. If a policy is obtained from the private carrier, the licensee must file a certificate of coverage with the KREC by the license renewal date of April 1st. Licenses expire on March 31st. The policy must conform to the KREC requirements and must contain a provision that the policy cannot be terminated, canceled, allowed to lapse, or not renewed without giving the KREC prior written notice.

The minimum coverage permissible is no less than $100,000 for any one claim nor less than $1,000,000 annual aggregate for all claims. Principal brokers may decide to purchase independent E&O "firm coverage." In that event, the aggregate amount shall be $1,000,000 annual aggregate for one to forty licensees and $2,000,000 annual aggregate for forty-one plus licensees. These amounts do not include legal defense and investigation costs. 201 KAR 11:220, Section 3(2).

Permissible deductibles are $2,500 for a judgment or settlement, and $1,000 for legal defense and investigation. 201 KAR 11:220, Section 3(3). Licensees may, in certain situations and with certain insurance companies, be able to obtain additional coverage amounts, lower deductibles, and endorsements that cover items excluded from the basic policy.

E & O policies are "claims made" policies. Because they are "claims made" policies, the policy in effect at the time the claim is filed against the licensee is the policy that must defend the claim. If the agent has one insurance company when the transaction occurs, but has a different policy when a lawsuit is filed, the policy in effect at the time the lawsuit is filed is the one that pays. Because these are "claims made" policies, a licensee is at risk of not having coverage if she changes insurance carriers without understanding there may be "a gap in coverage." If the licensee receives notice of a potential claim while with one insurance carrier and does not report the potential claim before changing insurance carriers, the new carrier does not have to provide coverage when the claim is actually filed. It is critical that, before changing insurance carriers, the licensee discusses this issue at length with the new carrier.

One of the biggest problems that licensees have with the E&O insurance policy is not reporting claims. Licensees always believe the problem will go away and if it does not, they will contact the carrier later. This is a huge mistake. E&O policies require notice of a claim as set forth in the policy. Licensees should review their policies to find out the notice requirements. If a licensee does not give timely notice, the carrier does not have to defend the claim. Many times the licensee thinks she can handle the problem and that only makes it worse. Always remember -- if someone says anything that makes you think they may file a lawsuit, KREC complaint, or professional standards complaint, notify the E&O carrier immediately!

Summary

To engage in real estate transactions for real property owned by another person requires a license issued by the Commonwealth of Kentucky. A real estate license enables the agent to transact business throughout the state of Kentucky. The licensee may choose to work with residential, commercial, industrial, and/or farm property. It is important to remember that property management is a licensed activity that must be conducted with the knowledge, consent, and participation of the licensee's principal broker. Licenses expire on March 31st annually. Not all licensees are REALTORS®.

Licensees must work under the direction of a principal broker who must adequately supervise all affiliates in his office. The principal broker may be the owner of the company or may be someone hired by the owner to act as principal broker. Although the KREC does not issue a special license for principal brokers, the KREC must be notified of the name of the principal broker and must be notified if there is a change. Principal brokers may terminate the licensee's affiliation without cause, and the licensee may change principal brokers at will.

Principal brokers may appoint someone with an associate's license or with a broker's license to act as a designated manager. This designation is recognized by the KREC and the designated manager is charged with adequately supervising licensees and performing all tasks assigned to her by the principal broker. The designated manager may be liable under the license law in the same way as the principal broker.

Owners may transact business relating to their own property without a license. There are other exceptions to the licensing requirement. An employee who is hired as a regular employee of the owner for the purpose of transacting business relating to the owner's real property does not need a license. A regular employee managing property for the owner, or the principal broker hired by the owner to manage property, does not need a license. An attorney-in-fact, transacting business for the owner under the authority of a power of attorney, does not need a license. Neither does a person acting under a court order that specifically authorizes real estate transactions. Attorneys-at-law need a real estate license when dealing with real estate they do not own, unless they are transacting real estate business in their capacity as an attorney for the owner. In order for the attorney to qualify for this exemption, the attorney may not be paid a commission.

A very limited exception to brokering real estate in Kentucky without a Kentucky real estate license relates to out-of-state brokers. Those brokers must enter into a written agreement with a Kentucky principal broker, and must work under the direct supervision of the Kentucky broker. KRS 324.235-KRS 324.238 should be reviewed by both the Kentucky principal broker and the out-of-state broker prior to entering into the written agreement. The statutes are very specific and must be followed exactly.

The license law allows unlicensed assistants, a/k/a non-licensed personal assistants, to perform limited duties relative to real estate transactions. They may contact the public to set appointments and may provide general public information. All activities of the unlicensed assistant must be under the direct supervision and control of the principal broker. Licensees utilizing unlicensed assistants should use caution to make sure the unlicensed assistant is not practicing real estate and that the public knows the assistant is unlicensed.

Licensees affiliated with real estate brokerages are usually independent contractors and not employees. As such, they are self-employed. The principal broker cannot require them to work certain hours and cannot require them to work in any certain way, as long as they comply with the law. Their share of the commissions earned are paid to them by the principal broker without income and social security taxes being deducted. It is the licensees' obligation to pay their own income and social security taxes when they become due.

To obtain a real estate license, a person has to be at least 18 years of age, must have at least a high school or G.E.D diploma, must be trustworthy and competent, must complete required education in real estate, and must pass a standardized multiple choice test. Additional education is required to obtain a broker's license, along with experience working in real estate. All applicants for a license must supply the KREC a criminal background check from the FBI or from any other commission-approved criminal background-checking provider or company furnishing identification records that are comparable to those provided by the FBI, as determined by the commission. 201 KAR 11:430.

Kentucky no longer offers Kentucky licenses by reciprocity. Currently, discussions are being held with the state of Ohio to decide whether or not Kentucky and Ohio may go back to reciprocity. "License recognition" has replaced reciprocity. The out-of-state licensee applicant must hold an active, unrestricted, sales associates or broker's license in another state. The applicant must (1) supply an FBI criminal background check; (2) file a certification of licensure issued by the regulatory agency in the state where he/she is licensed; (3) pass the Kentucky license law portion of the sales associates or brokers examination (depending on the type of license held in the other state); and (4) apply for the license within 60 days of passing the licensing examination.

Licensees who do not want to maintain an active license may place their license in escrow. They cannot transact real estate business while the license is in escrow, but they may re-activate the license without re-taking the examination.

Licensees are required to take six hours of continuing education each year, and three of those hours must be in real estate law. Every four years, licensees are required to take the Kentucky Core Class. In the event a licensee cannot complete the required continuing education classes, he may enter into a delinquency plan with the KREC by paying a $500 fine. The plan must be completed by June 15th. If the plan is not completed by June 15th, the licensee may request a hearing. Unless a hearing is requested, the license will be suspended for a period of six months. And, of course, while the license is suspended, the licensee cannot practice real estate.

Effective January 1, 2016, all new sales associate licensees must take 48-hours of post-licensing education within their first two years of active licensure. If the hours are not completed, unless the Commission extends the deadline for good cause shown, the license will be canceled.

Because of the KREC's concern that continuing education, pre-license, and post-license classes are of high quality, it has set standards for real estate schools, instructors, and classes. In order to teach the classes, the schools and instructors must meet and maintain these requirements. Each class and instructor is evaluated by the class attendees.

All licensees in Kentucky are required to carry errors and omissions insurance. The state provides a group policy, but the licensee may choose to use another insurance carrier. One of the biggest mistakes a licensee can make is failing to report a claim to the E&O carrier in a timely manner.

CHAPTER 2

BROKERAGE PRACTICES
Escrow Accounts, Offers and Contracts, Advertising, and Seller Disclosure of Property Condition

Statutes and Administration Regulations

Chapter Objectives

This chapter reviews the licensing statutes and regulations that govern **real estate brokerage** practices. Included in this chapter is specific information relating to the Principal Broker's escrow account and how it must be handled to comply with the law. Offers and contracts are addressed, with an emphasis on learning the importance of differentiating between an offer and a contract in the day-to-day practice of real estate. Advertising regulations are discussed with the goal of preventing KREC fines levied against the licensee for advertising violations. The Seller's Disclosure of Property Condition form is examined to give the licensee practical information on how to comply with the statute and regulation. Frequently asked questions that will be answered in Chapter 2 are:

1. How does a real estate brokerage operate?
2. What is an escrow account?
3. What happens to the buyer's earnest money deposit?
4. Can the Principal Broker commingle the escrow funds with general brokerage funds?
5. What is required for the Principal Broker to remove the earnest money from his/her escrow account?
6. Can the escrow account be interest bearing?
7. How must a written offer be handled?
8. What information must be included in the offer to purchase?
9. Who must sign the offer to purchase?
10. What information must be included in the listing contract?
11. Who must sign the listing contract?
12. Who owns the listing contract and the purchase contract?
13. What is a back-up offer?
14. What is a back-up contract?
15. Does the license law regulate brokerage advertising?
16. What are the advertising guidelines?
17. What must be included in every advertisement?
18. Are there specific rules for internet advertising?

Associations of REALTORS® are working with a third party company to assist in getting the earnest money from the buyer to the principal broker's escrow account. Although this sounds like a possible solution, the principal broker still remains liable under the licensing laws and regulations.

Another common problem involves depositing the money into a principal broker's escrow account while the contract is still being negotiated. This is a violation of the license law and can lead to a court action to get a court order to release the money when the buyer and seller refuse to sign a mutual release. The money is properly deposited when there is an executory contract, and not any sooner.

Release of Escrow Account Funds

Once escrow money is deposited into the escrow account, there are very strict guidelines for the **release of escrow account funds**. Those guidelines are set forth in KRS 324.111(3)(4)(6). First, a check may not be written to remove funds on uncollected deposits. When the principal broker deposits the check, he cannot write a check on his account until the check that was deposited clears his bank. It is important for the principal broker to know how long it takes a check to clear his account, and whether or not her bank places a hold on checks.

Problems arise when a check is deposited but does not clear the bank, because of either insufficient funds or stopped payment, and the principal broker has already written a check out of the account. Not only is the principal broker in violation of the licensing law, but she may also be required to use her personal funds to cover the check that did not clear. When a check does not clear the bank, the principal broker must notify the parties immediately upon receiving the information from the bank.

The statute sets forth four instances when it is appropriate to remove money from the principal broker's escrow account. KRS 324.111. These are the only times money may be removed under the statute. For many years the principal broker could remove the money from the broker's escrow account pursuant to the terms of the contract. This is no longer true. This statute was amended a few years ago.

If the principal broker removes escrowed funds at any other time, he may be sanctioned by the Kentucky Real Estate Commission, as well as facing penalties ordered by the Circuit Court, which may be not only civil in nature, but also criminal.

Contract Terminated by Performance When the contract is completed by performance (that is, when the transaction closes), the earnest money may be removed from the escrow account. Escrowed funds are disbursed at closing according to various practices prevailing in different areas of the state. Some principal brokers write a check from the escrow account directly to the buyer. In those cases the buyer endorses the check to the seller or to the settlement agent. Other principal brokers prefer to write the check to the seller, and the buyer receives credit on the settlement statement. Principal brokers in other areas of the state keep the deposit as part of their commission, and both the seller and buyer receive a credit on the closing statement. As long as all parties understand the process, agree to the disbursement, and have a paper trail, there is no problem with these different practices.

Mutual Agreement of the Parties Escrowed funds may be released by mutual agreement of all parties to the transaction. KRS 324.111(4). This situation arises when the sales contract is not going to close, and the parties mutually agree to release the deposit. Licensees must remember that releasing earnest money does not necessarily release the parties from obligations under the sales contract. In order to release the parties from the contract, a written release must specifically state that fact.

Because licensees are not parties to the contract, they are not required to sign the release in order to remove earnest money from the account. Many areas of the state have releases prepared by local associations and boards with blanks for the licensees to sign. Their signatures are not required to release the escrow funds; rather, they sign the release to relinquish their rights under the contract to receive a commission. Principal Brokers that do not want to release their rights to a commission under the contract should not sign the release. This is a common mistake that prevents the Principal Broker from filing a Broker's Lien against the property, and prevents other collection remedies for the Principal Broker.

Court Order Funds may be released from the escrow account upon the principal broker receiving a court order from a court of competent jurisdiction. KRS 324.111(4). Competent jurisdiction means that the court entering the order has the legal authority to do so. When the parties cannot mutually agree to release the money, one of them may file a court action to have the court determine how the principal broker will disburse the funds.

Because most earnest money deposits are less than $5,000, the cases are filed in either small claims court, if the amount is less than $2,500, or regular district court, if the amount is more than $2,500 and no more than $5,000. Cases involving commercial transactions, which tend to have much larger earnest money deposits, may be filed in state circuit court or in federal district court, depending on the situation that led to the court filing. Principal brokers may decide to file court actions to get the money released, or choose to wait until one of the parties moves the case into court.

Once a court order is received by the principal broker, he should not disburse the funds until the time for appeal has passed. In Kentucky, every court action may be appealed one time to a higher court. Each party has 30 days to file an appeal. If the funds are released before the 30-day period expires, and the higher court overturns the decision of the lower court, the principal broker will be in a position of recovering the money paid to the wrong person or paying the money himself. Neither option is a good one; either one may well lead to sanctions by the KREC for improperly releasing escrow funds.

Principal Broker 60-day Letter A statutory way to remove money from an escrow account may be initiated by the principal broker as set forth in KRS 324.111(6). This is a permissive statute, which means the principal broker may decide to follow this process or she may not. Because the statute uses the word "may" and not "shall," the principal broker is not required to move forward with the release process. Many principal brokers choose not to decide which party will receive the money and will wait until one of the parties decides to move the matter forward with litigation.

Once the principal broker receives notice from one of the parties that the transaction is not going to close, she may initiate the release process. To initiate the process, she sends a letter by certified mail to the last known address of the parties. In this notice, she informs the parties how she intends to disburse the money if they do not sign a mutual release, or if one, or more, of them do not institute court action. The notice gives the parties 60 days from the mailing date on the letter to act before she releases the money as set forth in the letter.

When the 60 days pass, the principal broker may release the money as set forth in the letter. Once the money is released, as long as the process was followed properly, the principal broker will not be liable to the parties, even if one or both of them file a complaint with the KREC or with the circuit court.

Property Management Funds

Principal brokers that manage rental property for others must either have a separate account for the property management escrow funds, or they must indicate in all records for the brokerage escrow account which funds belong to property management clients. KRS 324.111(7). Unless the brokers and sales associates affiliated with a principal broker are required by the principal broker to deposit property management funds into the brokerage escrow for property they personally own, they are not required by the licensing law to use the principal broker's escrow account. KRS 324.111(8).

KREC Emergency Action

KRS 324.111(9) gives the KREC the right to conduct an emergency hearing when it is alleged that a licensee has violated the law relating to the principal broker's escrow account. In the past when the KREC learned of an alleged violation it had to use the process outlined in KRS 324.151. This led to long delays in the investigation, although it was an emergency situation. Now, the KREC can conduct an emergency hearing pursuant to KRS 324.150(1)(b). At the time of printing this text, the KREC is in the process of writing the regulation that outlines the process to be followed for an emergency hearing.

****

Case: Improper Handling of Escrow Account Case

In re: William D. James, Debtor, David W. Bailey and William H. Grissom, Plaintiffs vs. William D. James, Defendant, United State Bankruptcy Court for the Western District of Kentucky, 42 B. R. 265 (1984)

The debtor in this bankruptcy case, William D. James, was a real estate broker. Mr. James will be referred to as James. He and the other plaintiffs in this case, David Bailey and William Grissom, were real estate brokers who had a partnership known as Bailey and Grissom Real Estate Brokers. The partnership will be referred to as B & G.

James and B & G entered into an auction contract with the heirs of the Andy Garvin Estate to sell the Beech Bend Amusement Park and surrounding acreage in Bowling Green, Kentucky. They agreed that they would share equally in the expenses and the profits of the sale. James would keep all money collected in his escrow account and the expenses would be paid through that account.

B & G borrowed $20,000.00 from American National Bank and Trust Company to be used to promote and advertise the property. James and B & G signed the note and each agreed to repay 50% through James' escrow account from the sales commissions earned on the sale of the property.

The original sales date of October 4, 1977, was postponed because of a dispute among the heirs. Warren Circuit Court set a new sales date for February 3, 1978, and ordered James and B & G to be paid $20,000.00 for advertising costs related to the cancelled sale. On February 3, 1978, the property sold for $1,449,000.00 and the two firms were paid a total of $62,450.00 in real estate commission and advertising expenses.

James placed the $62,450.00 in his escrow account. James was to pay himself $14,000.43 for commission and B & G was to receive $14,000.44. $34,449.13 was to be used to pay the American National Bank loan and the remaining sale expenses. On September 20, 1978, James prepared a statement entitled "Garvin Commission Disbursement" that showed payments of $20,000.00 to the American Bank, $2,299.13 interest on escrow rebate, $2,000.00 for surveying, $150.00 for ground preparation, $10,000.00 for advertising, and $14,000.44 to B & G, and $14,000.43 to James, for a total expenditure of $62,450.00.

It was later discovered that the $20,000.00 had not been paid on the bank note. After being contacted by B & G, James paid $10,000 on the note on January 30, 1979, and paid other interest payments prior to filing bankruptcy. On April 8, 1981, B & G filed a complaint with the Kentucky Real Estate Commission to collect the $10,000.00 from the Kentucky Real Estate Commission Education Research and Recovery fund. A hearing was held, but, for some reason not noted by the Court, the case was dismissed by the KREC.

On April 21, 1981, James filed a petition for bankruptcy. The bank, that was still owed $11,010.49, filed suit against James and B & G in October of 1981. B & G paid the bank note. B & G filed an action against James, alleging that he had embezzled the funds and objecting to the debt to the bank being discharged in his bankruptcy. If the bank was discharged, B & G would never have been able to collect from James.

To prove that James had embezzled the money, B & G had to prove that James appropriated the money for his own benefit and that he did so with fraudulent intent or deceit. Both the intent and actual misappropriation may be proven by circumstantial evidence.

The bankruptcy court considered the record and concluded that James' actions did constitute embezzlement. James admitted that he received the payments due B & G and also due his company (Bill James & Associates), and admitted that he agreed to repay the bank loan and failed to do so after assuring B & G he would pay the loan. Based on the admissions by James, the Court believed it was clearly shown that James intentionally and knowingly breached the agreement with B & G to pay the bank note. Although James defended by stating his failure to pay was caused by poor health and ill-fated investments, the Court concluded that the debt in question was non-dischargeable in his bankruptcy. Because the debt was not dischargeable, B & G has a right to collect the debt in the future.

Apparently, the reason the Court believed James had embezzled the funds was that he constantly assured B & G the debt would be paid. Typically, embezzlement would not be found if the funds were used openly for their own purposes without attempting to conceal the funds.

Another important point made by the court was that this case was for a limited purpose of determining a bankruptcy issue and not for resolving all issues that may be brought in another court relating to the misappropriation of funds.

****

Offers and Counteroffers

Offers to purchase property in real estate transactions are made by the buyer, known as the **offeror**, to the seller, known as the **offeree**. Occasionally, the seller will make the initial offer to the buyer, in which event the seller would be the offeror and the buyer would be the offeree. Usually, however, an offer by the seller comes in the form of a **counteroffer** in response to the offer by the buyer. The counteroffer from the seller makes changes in the terms offered by the buyer. Of course, a further counteroffer may then be made by the buyer, changing the seller's terms. Each time a counteroffer is more about value of property, net listings may lead some agents not to tell the seller the actual value of the property when listing it for sale.

The property listed must be described so that that principal broker knows what she is listing, and the seller knows what he is selling. Street address, legal description, plat reference, mailing address, or anything else that sufficiently describes the real estate may be used. A copy of the deed may be attached to the listing for clarification.

All owners must sign the listing. The listing licensee should ask herself at the time of listing: "who must sign the deed at closing?" If any one of those people do not sign the listing, there is no listing. Without a listing the licensee cannot advertise the property, including, but not limited to, having a sign in the yard. The principal broker is not entitled to a commission even if he sells the property. A person who has not signed the listing will not be forced by the courts to sell the property or pay a commission. Often agents believe that it is enough if one spouse or one joint owner signs the listing. That is not true. When dealing with a court appointee, i.e. trustee, executor, or guardian, that person, with proper court order, is considered the seller. If a power of attorney is being used, the attorney-in-fact under the power of attorney is considered the owner. The basic rule is: "all owners must sign the listing -- no exception." (Author's note: I recently published a small booklet that outlines in detail who must sign the listings when the property is part of an estate or sold with someone using a power of attorney. *"Don't Let Wills, Estates, and Trusts Be the Death of You!"* Copies are available directly from the author or fromAmazon.com.)

Special showing instructions must also be included in the contract. Although it may not be conducive to a quick sale, the seller has a right to limit the times and days his property may be shown. Those restrictions are legal and must be followed by the principal broker, her affiliates, and any cooperating brokers and their affiliates that may show the property. Failure to follow these legal instructions may subject the licensee to sanctions by the KREC and possibly to legal action in the court system for breach of fiduciary duty. Licensees must examine special showing instructions to ensure the seller is not trying to violate the fair housing laws. If a licensee determines the special instructions are for the purpose of discrimination, the prudent principal broker and associate will not take the listing.

Subagency restrictions are also required to be stated in the listing contract. The listing contract creates an agency relationship between the seller and the principal broker. In many instances, the listing principal broker agrees to cooperate with other principal brokers to allow the agents of that principal broker to show the property. In those situations, the cooperating broker, and his agents, may either represent the seller as the subagent of the listing broker, may represent the buyer as a buyer's agent, or may represent no one and act as a transaction broker. If the cooperating broker acts as a subagent, he and his agents will also be representing the seller, along with the listing principal broker. Because of the issue of legal liability, many sellers do not want to be represented by subagents. In that event, the listing contract must state that cooperating brokers must be either buyer's agents or transaction brokers.

If a seller and principal broker agree to make changes to the listing contract, they may do so by entering into a new listing contract, or by amending the original contract. When the seller and broker choose to amend the contract by making changes on the original contract, all changes must be initialed by the parties, and each initial must have the date and time that it was written.

Back-Up Contracts

A buyer may want to make an offer on a property that already has a sales contract, but has not closed. Because the property has already sold, the seller cannot accept another offer, but the seller may accept an offer that creates a "**back-up contract**."

A back-up contract is one that becomes the primary contract if and when the first contract terminates without closing. This might occur, for example if the first buyer can not obtain mortgage financing to purchase the property. If the sales contract was contingent upon the buyer obtaining financing, the seller must release the first buyer from the contract. When the first contract is released, the buyer with the back-up contract becomes the primary buyer and may purchase the property.

Back-up offers and back-up sales contracts often lead to disputes. Because of potential problems with this situation, Section 3 of 201 KAR 11:250 was written with specific language that must be used when writing a back-up offer. That language is: "This offer is submitted as a back-up offer, which means the property is subject to a previously-accepted offer which has priority over this offer." The language attempts to make clear that the back-up offer, once accepted, may only then become a back-up contract. This language must be included in the offer if the licensee writing the offer knows that the property is already under contract. If the language is not in the offer, it must be inserted by the listing agent and treated as a counteroffer.

In back-up offer situations, it should be made clear to the buyer that they are entering into a sales/purchase contract, and they must perform if the primary contract is released prior to closing. Back-up buyers often continue to look for property and are disappointed when they find another property, but cannot make an offer on it because of the existence of the back-up contract which obligates them to perform if the first buyer fails to perform and obtains a release fro the seller. Back-up contracts are not back-up options which give the buyer the "option" of closing the transaction. A back-up contract is a contract that must be performed if the primary contract is released.

Advertising

Advertising is one of the most important functions of real estate brokerage. This is the mechanism used to create goodwill for the company, recruit new agents, and market real estate to sellers and buyers, both inside and outside of Kentucky. Brokerages use written, oral, and electronic means of advertising in an effort to reach wide audiences. Because of the potential for misuse of advertising in the real estate industry, the licensing laws and regulations have very specific requirements. And, of course, the principal broker, or someone designated by the principal broker, must approve all advertisements that are placed by the licensees affiliated with the brokerage. 201 KAR 11:105, Section 4(1).

The license law provides that the name of a deceased principal broker may remain in the firm name. KRS 324.117(2). A sales associate may have his or her name as part of the brokerage name after having two (2) years with the company averaging at least twenty (20) hours per week for twenty-four (24) months. KRS 324.117(3)

KRS 324.117(1) states that real estate advertising shall not be intentionally false, misleading or deceptive. As defined by 201 KAR 11:011(3), false, misleading, or deceptive advertising as "an advertisement that is prohibited . . . because the advertisement (a) [c]ontrary to fact, (b) [l]eads a person to a mistaken belief or conclusion; or (c) [k]nowingly made a presentation that is contrary to fact." False advertising is advertising that is simply untrue. Misleading advertising may be true, but is phrased in such a way that the reader reaches a false conclusion. Deceptive advertising is known to be false when the advertisement is placed and it is used with the intention of misleading the consumer.

When prosecuting a case against a licensee for an advertising violation, the KREC has the burden of proving the advertisement placed by the licensee was *intentionally* false, misleading, or deceptive. Prior versions of this statute did not have the word "intentional," which led to licensees being sanctioned when they accidentally, negligently, or unknowingly, had a false, misleading, or deceptive advertisement. Although the burden of proof for the KREC is higher than it has been in the past, a prudent licensee will take care to make sure their ads are not false, misleading, or deceptive.

A licensee must have the written consent of the owner to publicly promote listed property. Because placing a sign on the property is considered public promotion, the licensee must have the owner's written permission to place the sign. 201 KAR 11:105. This permission is usually contained in the listing contract. Once the listing contract has expired or the property has sold and closed, the principal broker must remove the sign because she no longer has written permission to have the sign on the property. In some areas of Kentucky, agents want to leave the sign in the yard to promote their business by showing they sold the property. After the closing, the licensee must have written permission of the new owner to leave the sign on the premises.

Licensees must advertise in the name of their principal broker or company name as shown on their license. If the principal broker's name is used, the principal broker's title of "Principal Broker" must be included in the advertisement. 201 KAR 11:105, Section 3. The exception to this rule is if the licensee is advertising, for sale or lease, property he personally owns. With the principal broker's permission, the licensee's personally owned property may be advertised without the broker or company name. KRS 324.117(4).

At the time of publication of this book there was much discussion on how prominent the name of the principal broker or company had to be in advertising, particularly on signs. Many licensees want their name larger and more noticeable than the company or principal broker's name. Licensees are encouraged to follow these discussions, contact the KREC with input, and take the time to learn the final outcome of these discussions prior to having signs printed and websites created and/or changed.

Once property is listed, owners who advertise their own listed property must follow the advertising laws that require the name of the listing brokerage or the name of the principal broker with her title of "Principal Broker." Licensees must inform the owners of this requirement in writing, obtain the owners written agreement that they will follow the law, and keep a copy of the notice in their file. KRS 324.117(4) and 201 KAR 11:105, Section 4(2). With the use of social media to advertise their properties, owners are often running afoul of this law. Owners should be informed that postings on Facebook, Linked-in, and other similar sites, are considered advertisements.

A licensee may advertise public information about properties that he did not have listed. For example, this information may include the sales price or the fact that a property sold and closed. Agents often use this information to compare their brokerage sales performance with the performance of another brokerage. The key to this regulation is that the information must be public information. 201 KAR 11:105(5).

201 KAR 11:105(1)(2)(a) provides that a buyer's agent may advertise or promote her participation in the sale after a closing has occurred. The advertising must make it clear that the licensee was acting as the buyer's agent.

With the advent of various software products that allow brokerages to advertise each other's listings, 201 KAR 11:105(6), was amended to permit this type of advertising. A licensee may advertise listings of another brokerage if the listing broker consents to the advertisement and if the advertisement includes the complete name of the listing brokerage. The consumer must be informed that the property is not listed by the company advertising it.

Internet Advertising

With the explosion of **internet advertising**, the Kentucky Real Estate Commission, the state and federal Attorneys General, the Courts, and numerous other regulatory agencies are being bombarded with issues. The internet really is the "wild west." Licensees should carefully weigh where and how they choose to advertise on the internet to make sure they are advertising within the law. Web sites need to be maintained regularly. Failure to update a web site can easily lead to false and misleading advertising. Because web sites can be accessed by unauthorized people and entities (an eight year old working out of her bedroom, for example), licensees should monitor their web sites regularly.

Key Terms

A review of the key terms prior to reading this chapter will assist you in understanding the license law relating to material in the chapter. It is always important to know how a certain word, term, or phrase is used in the particular statute or regulation you are studying. You will learn that sometimes a word, term, or phrase means something different from statute to statute. Each word is highlighted in the text the first time it appears in the chapter. There is a comprehensive Glossary in the back of the book.

Affiliated Licensees	Agency by Estoppel
Agency by Ratification	Agency Disclosure Form
Agent	Business Relationship
Buyer Agency	Client
Commercial Property	Confidential Information
Contact	Cooperating Broker
Customer	Delivery
Designated Agency	Dual Agent
Duty of Accounting	Duty of Confidentiality
Duty of Disclosure	Duty of Loyalty
Duty of Obedience to Lawful Instructions	Duty of Reasonable Care and Diligence
Express Agency	Family Relationship
Fiduciary Duties	Implied Agency
In-house Transaction	Limited Agent
Material Facts	Multiple Listing Service (MLS)
Operation of Law	Ostensible Agency
Party	Personal Assistant
Personal Relationship	Principal
Principal Broker	Prospective Party
Sales Associate	Scope of Authority
Seller Agency	Special Agent
Statute of Frauds	Sub-agency
Supervising Licensee	Transaction Broker
Undisclosed Agency	Unlicensed Assistant

Affiliated Licensees: Real estate licensees that are associated with a particular real estate brokerage and the principal broker is said to "hold" their licenses. Sometimes referred to as agents or associates.

Agency by Estoppel: An agency relationship created when the principal and agent act in such a way to lead a third party to believe an agency relationship exists. Basically, if two parties act as though they are principal and agent they are "stopped" from denying that relationship later. Also referred to as ostensible agency.

Agency by Ratification: Form of agency created when an agent acts on behalf of a principal without authority to do so, and the principal chooses to affirm the agent's actions.

Agency Disclosure Form: KREC required form disclosing the agency relationship in the transaction that is prepared for the buyer when an offer is written and for the seller when the offer is presented.

Agent: A person authorized to represent the interests of, and perform certain acts on behalf of, another person in dealings with a third party. The person represented is known as the principal, and the agent owes fiduciary duties to the principal.

Business Relationship: This term is used in conjunction with Parts 1 and 2 of the Agency Disclosure form required by the KREC. When completing either Part 1 or Part 2 of the form, the licensee must indicate if an ongoing business relationship with another party to the transaction exists and/or if he has ever been involved in a prior real estate transaction with another party to the transaction.

Buyer Agency: The agency relationship existing between the licensee and the buyer where the licensee represents the buyer and no one else in the transaction. In this relationship, the licensee owes fiduciary duties only to the buyer.

Client: The party in an agency relationship who is represented by the agent. May also be referred to as the principal.

Commercial Property: This phrase is commonly used to refer to non-residential income producing properties, although it may be applied to apartment complexes. For licensee purposes, commercial property is defined in 201 KAR 11:400 as property other than a single-family residential lot or dwelling, agricultural property, or multi-family property containing less than four units.

Confidential Information: As used in the licensing law, any information that would materially compromise the negotiating position of either party to the transaction.

Contact: When used in the licensing law, a discussion or correspondence between a licensee and another person relating to the licensee's brokerage services.

Cooperating Broker: When the listing principal broker permits another principal broker to sell or lease her listed property, the principal broker bringing the buyer or tenant to the transaction is known as the cooperating broker or "co-op." The cooperating broker has no contractual relationship with the seller or owner of the property and is paid his/her commission by the listing broker. On occasion, the co-op is paid by his buyer client.

Customer: In real estate transactions, the person who is not represented by an agent is known as the customer.

Delivery: This term has several different meanings in real estate law. The term may be used to indicate that a written document has actually been delivered to a person as required by the licensing laws. Examples of delivery include delivering the sellers disclosure of property condition (KRS 324.360), delivering the agency disclosure form (KRS 201 KAR 11:400), and the delivery of all forms signed by a party in a real estate transaction (201 KAR 11:090). Actual delivery of documents in other real property contexts require that certain documents be delivered from one party to the other to consummate the transaction. These situations require the grantor to deliver the deed to the grantee to convey title and the mortgagor to deliver the mortgage to the mortgagee to convey a lien interest.

Designated Agency: Under the license law, a principal broker, in an in-house sale, may appoint one agent to represent the seller and one agent to represent the buyer. The licensing statute sets forth specific instructions on how the designation must occur, and it requires the principal broker to remain a limited dual agent, representing both the seller and buyer.

Dual Agent: In a real estate transaction in which the principal broker and all of her agents represents both the seller and the buyer.

Duty of Accounting: The fiduciary duty of the agent to inform the principal about all monies received and disbursed by the agent on behalf of the principal.

Duty of Confidentiality: The fiduciary duty of the agent to keep all of the principal's personal information confidential. These confidences must be kept not only during the representation, but they must be kept secret forever.

Duty of Disclosure: The fiduciary duty of the agent to inform the principal about all material facts surrounding the property and the transaction. This duty extends not only to the physical condition of the real property, but also to any fact that would affect the principal's decisions regarding the purchase or sale of the property.

Duty of Loyalty: The fiduciary duty of the agent to protect the interests of the principal above the interests of all others, including those of the agent.

Duty of Obedience to Lawful Instructions: The fiduciary duty of the agent to follow all legal instructions of the principal even if the agent does not agree with the instructions.

Duty of Reasonable Care and Diligence: The fiduciary duty of the agent to use at least the same level of skill and effort in representing the principal as another agent would use.

Express Agency: An expressed agreement, either oral or written, in which the principal and agent agree to create an agency relationship. This is the opposite of an implied agency which is created by the actions of the principal or agent.

In the event of a dispute as to whether or not an agency relationship actually exists, the burden to prove that agency exists, and the extent of the agent's authority under the agency, is on the person claiming that it does exist. *Jobe v. Witten*, 305 Ky. 457, 204 S.W.2d 575 (1947). This may become an issue in a dispute between the principal and agent, and may also become an issue in a dispute involving a third party who claims they acted in reliance on the agency relationship.

Agency by estoppel, sometimes referred to as **ostensible agency**, is created by **operation of law** when the principal acts as though the relationship exists and those actions lead a third party to reasonably believe it exists. *Beaver Dam Grain, Inc.*, Bkrtcy. Ky., 43 F.R. 283(1984). Ostensible agency gives rise to apparent authority or implied. If the third party relies on the apparent authority and is damaged, the principal cannot deny that an agency relationship existed. *Mill Street Church of Christ v. Hogan*, Ky.App., 785 S.W.2d 263 (1990).

Because the relationship is created by two parties, the testimony of only one party that the relationship exists is not enough. *Lanham v. Felts*, 306 Ky. 851, 209 S.W.2d 472 (1948). Facts and circumstances surrounding the relationship must be examined if the parties do not agree that the relationship existed. Agency may also be established when the agent and principal categorically deny the relationship based on facts and circumstances. *Carey-Reed Co. v. Hart*, 245 Ky. 325, 53 S.W.2d 689 (1932). Existence of the relationship becomes a question in real estate transactions not only in trying to determine if the agent is owed a fee, but also, and probably more often, in relation to liability issues. In a lawsuit, when the parties cannot agree if the relationship existed, the question is one that must be determined by the jury. *Crump v. Sabath*, 261 Ky. 652, 88 S.W.2d 665 (1936).

Agency may be created by ratification. Agency by ratification occurs when the principal affirms the actions taken on his behalf by someone who was not his agent at the time the action was taken. In essence, the agency relationship is created after-the-fact. *Stewart v. Mitchell's Adm'x.*, 301 Ky. 123, 190 S.W.2d 660 (1946). Once ratified, the agency relationship carries with it the same responsibilities, duties, and liabilities that it would have had it been created before the action was taken by the agent.

Termination

Like all legal relationships, the agency relationship will terminate at some point. The agency relationship may be terminated by: (1) completion of purpose for which the agency was created; (2) mutual agreement of the principal and agent; (3) revocation by principal or agent; (4) expiration of the term of the agency agreement; (5) destruction or condemnation of the property; (6) death or incapacity of either party; and (7) operation of law. In a real estate transaction, where the licensee is retained by the seller to list and sell a property, or retained by the buyer to locate a property, once the transaction is closed, the agency terminates. The principal and agent may also mutually agree to terminate the agency contract prior to the purpose of the agency being completed. In this event, the agent may negotiate compensation for time and expenses prior to the termination. Either party may terminate the relationship, but may be liable to the other party for damages. *Baumer v. Franklin County Distilling Co.,* C.C.A.Ky., 135 F.2d 384 (1943).

Well drafted agency contracts will contain an expiration date. Under Kentucky licensing law, listing contracts must contain an expiration date and that date may not be automatically extended. 201 KAR 11:250. If the contract does not contain an expiration date, whether or not the relationship has terminated is a question of fact for a jury to determine.

If the property that is the subject of the agency relationship is destroyed, the agency relationship ends. Because the agent was retained to sell or lease real estate and its improvements, once the real estate and/or its improvements no longer exists, there is no reason for the agency to continue. However, the agent may be entitled to compensation for services and reimbursement of expenses, if the seller acted in bad faith leading to the destruction of the property.

Because the agency relationship is a personal relationship, the death or incapacity of either the agent or principal will terminate the relationship. If a property is listed for sale and the principal broker dies or becomes incapacitated, the listing contract terminates. However, if the **sales associate**, who listed the property on behalf of the broker dies or becomes incapacitated, the listing does not terminate because the broker, not the sales associate, is the agent of the principal. Should the seller die or become incapacitated, the listing contract terminates unless the personal representative of the estate chooses to continue with the contract.

Agency can be terminated by "operation of law." The term "operation of law" simply means that there is a provision in the law that will override another provision of the law. An example arises when a person files bankruptcy. Although he has entered into an agency agreement to sell his real estate, the bankruptcy law provides that once someone files a bankruptcy petition, the trustee for the bankrupt estate determines which contracts will be honored. Another situation would be a seller who lists the property "for sale" then stops making mortgage payments, resulting in a foreclosure action. The foreclosure action may continue without regard to the agency relationship between the seller and the broker.

Types of Agency

Historically, in real estate transactions, all agents in the transaction represented the seller, and the buyer was not represented by any of the agents. The recent trend nationally, as well as in Kentucky, is for the principal broker to determine what agency relationships will be offered to consumers who work with his office. Most brokerages offer representation to buyer and sellers, while others offer representation only to sellers or only to buyers.

Seller Agency When a seller's agency is created, the seller is the "principal" and the principal broker and his affiliated licensees are the "agents" of the seller. In a seller agency relationship, the agent owes fiduciary duties to the seller.

A seller agency relationship in Kentucky is generally created by the listing contract. Under the license law, a listing must be in writing. However, under contract law the seller and agent may enter into an oral agreement for the agent to sell property. There is a conflict between the license law and contract law, and the prudent agent will follow the license law.

At least three problems may be created by the creation of an oral seller agency relationship. The license law requires a written listing before the property may be promoted or advertised to the general public. 201 KAR 11:105, Section 1. It is difficult to sell property without promoting and advertising it.

Secondly, a problem with an oral agreement between the broker and seller involves collection of the real estate commission. If the seller agrees to pay his agent a commission and actually makes the payment, the agent may legally accept it. However, if the seller decides not to pay the commission, and the agent only has an oral seller agency agreement, the agent cannot enforce the agreement.

Not part of the license law, but an important statute for licensees, is KRS 371.010, commonly referred to as the **Statute of Frauds**. This is the statute that requires a signed written agreement between the seller and principal broker, or the buyer and principal broker, before the principal broker can enforce his right to collect a commission. The statute says in pertinent part: "No action shall be brought to charge any person...(8) Upon any promise, agreement, or contract for any commission or compensation for the sale or lease of any real estate or for assisting another in the sale or lease of any real estate." This statute makes it clear that there must be a written agreement between the parties before the principal broker can enforce his right to collect the commission.

The license law requires that any agreement for compensation from a licensee to his or her client or customer shall be in writing. If a licensee fails to comply with the requirement in this section, the licensee's conduct shall be considered improper and in violation of KRS 324.160(4)(u).

Sub-agency When a seller's agent agrees to cooperate with another office and permit the licensees in that office to show his listing, the cooperating office may act either as a subagent or buyer's agent. If the cooperating agent acts as a subagent that means he is also representing the seller and not representing the buyer. Until the development of buyer agency and **designated agency**, the typical relationship between the seller and the cooperating agent was that of subagent. The subagent owes the seller the same fiduciary duties as the listing agent. *Capurso v. Johnson*, Ky., 248 S.W.2d 908 (1952). Like all agency relationships, the seller must consent to the creation of sub-agency. Kentucky administrative regulation 201 KAR 11:250, Section 1(7) sets forth requirements for the must be presumed that the Court of Appeals would have reached the same conclusion if the ASK agent had been a buyer's agent. This case was settled without a trial after being remanded to the Kenton Circuit Court; therefore, the issue of sub-agency vs. buyer agency was not decided by a jury. To date, there is no other Kentucky case that has specifically decided the issue.

****

Unlicensed Assistants

A relatively recent trend in real estate brokerage staff is the use of **unlicensed assistants**, or as they are referred to in the regulation, **Personal Assistants**. Unlicensed assistants are being used to perform many tasks once performed by licensed agents. Their use has led to controversy not only in the licensing regulatory agencies, but also among brokers and sales associates. Some feel that all brokerage work interacting with the consumer should require a license, while others believe the unlicensed assistant is capable of performing the service without harming the consumer. Although they were not widely used throughout the state, there is a growing trend to use more unlicensed assistants particularly in larger brokerages.

Kentucky's licensing law allows the use of unlicensed assistants. KRS 324.030(6) states: "A non-licensed person under the supervision of a licensed real estate broker who contacts the public for the purpose of setting an appointment for the broker to meet with them regarding buying or selling property and giving out general public information specifically authorized by the broker."

Pursuant to the statute, the Kentucky Real Estate Commission drafted administrative regulations to interpret this statute. The administrative regulation found in 201 KAR 11:440, specifically lists duties that may be performed by unlicensed assistants and duties that may not be performed. Included in the category of unlicensed assistants are not only someone hired with that title, but also office staff and clerical staff -- basically, anyone who is unlicensed who helps a licensee perform real estate services.

Section 1 of the regulation lists what work non-licensed personnel shall not perform. They may not "negotiate terms of a real estate transaction or real estate brokerage agreement." This prohibits them from negotiating sales contracts, listing contracts, buyer broker contracts, property management agreements, and leases.

Unlicensed personnel may not "complete offers or contracts relative to the real estate transaction." Real estate brokers and sales associates may complete form offers and contracts for listing and selling property. Although Kentucky considers completing these forms the unauthorized practice of law, the Kentucky Bar Association permits licensees to complete forms in the regular course of their business. Licensees may not draft legal documents. The interpretation of this regulation has changed since the regulation was adopted. At first the non-licensed person could not complete the form even if the licensee was dictating to them what was to be written in the blanks. Now, the interpretation allows the unlicensed person to fill out the form as long as the licensee is telling him what to write in each blank. Basically, now the assistant may act as the scrivener as long as he doesn't make the decision on what to write.

An unlicensed employee may not "disclose information that is available to a real estate licensee but is not available to the general public." This section requires the employee to keep the client's information confidential. The licensee must make the determination of what information may be disclosed to the public and what information may not be disclosed.

When discussions began in the real estate industry regarding this regulation, there was a movement to allow unlicensed assistants to attend the real estate closing without the licensee. However, the regulation that was approved does not allow the unlicensed person to "attend a real estate closing except to assist a licensee present at the closing." Interestingly enough, the license law does not require a licensee to attend his closing. Most agents believe attending the closing is an important part of their practice, but some do not feel it important to attend. If the broker or sales associate handling the transaction chooses not to attend, their unlicensed assistant may not attend.

201 KAR 11:440 attempts to set forth the duties that may be performed by an unlicensed assistant. Section 1 sets forth what an unlicensed person may not do: (1) negotiate terms of a transaction or other real estate agreement; (2) complete offers and contracts; (3) disclose information not available to the public; (4) attend a closing without a licensee; (5) access information from a trade association unless the **supervising licensee** is a member; (6) write or place ads without licensee review; (7) express material opinions about the real estate except to supervising licensee; (8) interpret real estate contracts for others; (9) represent that she has a license; (10) perform activities requiring a license.

Section 2 lists the tasks that may be performed by an unlicensed person working for a real estate brokerage. If the seller agrees, in writing, the unlicensed assistant may attend an open house with the supervising licensee. At the open house, she may distribute literature, serve refreshments, greet guests, and ask for signatures on a guest register. The unlicensed assistant may not "show" the house to prospective buyers attending the open house. Interpreting the word "show" has proven to be difficult. This is one section of the regulation that is still open to interpretation and debate.

The non-licensed person may provide orally a limited amount of information to consumers. He may state whether or not a particular piece of real estate is listed with the company and the listing price, whether or not there is a contract for the purchase of the property, and whether or not the transaction is closed. Although these basic questions may be answered, specific details may not be provided. Other information, with the supervising licensee's approval, may be provided by the assistant, but only in writing.

With the approval of the principal broker and supervising licensee, the unlicensed assistant's picture may appear in advertising as long as it is clear she does not have a license. She may receive confidential information from a client, but may disclose the information only to the supervising licensee. The assistant may also have keys copied.

One activity that still creates debate is allowing an unlicensed assistant to open the property for a third party. The regulation states that with the owner's consent an unlicensed assistant may open the property for any purpose relative to the transaction. However, while opening the property, the unlicensed assistant may not answer questions about it or show the property. The regulation does not say written consent is required, but a prudent licensee would certainly want the consent in writing. Some read the regulation to mean that the assistant may open the door for the appraiser, home inspector, and others working on "the transaction." Others believe the door may be opened to anyone who wants to enter, including prospective buyers, without the necessity of there being a "transaction." Clearly, an unlicensed assistant opening the door for a prospect without a licensee being present is a very risky proposition. Agents should consult with their principal broker and managers about the office policy on this regulation. Principal Brokers should consult legal counsel before deciding how to proceed.

The assistant may also contact consumers to set appointments for the supervising licensee. It appears that the unlicensed assistant may "telemarket" and "cold call" for the licensee. Cold calling means that the assistant may go door to door soliciting appointments for the supervising licensee. Although not specifically required in the regulation, the Kentucky Real Estate Commission recommends that the supervising licensee write a script that must be used in telemarketing and cold calling. And, of course, the supervising licensee must always be available to answer questions, and the assistant must always make it clear they do not have a real estate license.

If the principal broker allows unlicensed assistants to work in the office, he must assign a supervising licensee to manage the assistants. The broker must also require the assistants to understand the law and provide training for them. Supervising licensees must provide reasonable supervision of the assistants and must be reasonably accessible to the assistants. However the regulation does not define "reasonable supervision," or "reasonably accessible." The broker must provide "adequate supervision" and it is unclear if the KREC defines "reasonable" and "adequate" to be the same level of supervision.

One issue that has had various interpretations is the way unlicensed assistants may be compensated. At one point, it was stated that the assistants had to be employed. Then, at another point, they could be independent contractors. And, yet, at another point the interpretation was that they could be compensated based on the number of real estate transactions they participated in as long as the principal broker did not split commissions with unlicensed parties. Because of the evolving interpretation of the compensation issue, it is suggested that the principal broker contact the Kentucky Real Estate Commission directly to discuss this issue.

Property Management

Although most Kentucky licensees list and sell real estate, many also manage real property that is being leased. Property management may be part of the brokerage's activity, along with listing and selling, or it may be the only licensed activity conducted by the company. Some licensees represent only the property owners, while some choose to represent prospective tenants.

The definition of property management in the licensing statute is very broad. KRS 324.010(9) defines property management as:

> ...the overall management of real property for others for a fee, compensation, or other valuable consideration, and may include the marketing of property, the leasing of property, collecting rental payments on the property, payment of notes, mortgages, and other debts on the property, coordinating maintenance of the property, remitting funds and accounting statements to the owner and other activities that the commission may determine by administrative regulation.

Basically, the regulation considers anyone who receives something of value for performing tasks relating to someone else's rental property as being engaged in property management. This is a very broad definition, and includes many services that people perform every day without a license. It's safe to say that this one issue could keep the KREC busy everyday if they had the manpower. The unlicensed practice of property management is a huge problem.

If someone manages property for another, a real estate license is required -- with two exceptions. KRS 324.020(2). Those two exceptions are included in KRS 324.030(5), and are: (1) a regular employee of the owner or principal broker of the company retained to manage the property, and (2) someone who receives as primary compensation the use of a rental unit." A "regular employee" is defined in KRS 324.010(12), as "an employee who works for an employer whose total compensation is subject to withholding of federal and state taxes and FICA payments, and who received from the employer a fixed salary governed by federal wage guidelines that is not affected by specific real estate transactions." Someone managing real property without a license cannot be compensated based on the units leased or tenants procured.

Because licensees managing property often have money that belongs to the owner and/or the tenant, the principal broker must have a system operating in the office that keeps that money separate and apart from other brokerage funds. Property management funds may be kept in a separate escrow account, or they may be kept in the brokerage's general escrow account. If the funds are kept in the general escrow account, it must be clearly stated in the escrow account records which funds are specifically for property management. KRS 324.111(7).

One continuing problem is affiliates practicing property management without their principal broker's knowledge, consent, and assistance. A property management agreement is just like a listing agreement -- it belongs to the principal broker and must be handled through the office. The affiliate cannot manage real property for third parties without the principal broker's involvement. With the principal broker's agreement, an affiliate may manage his personally-owned real estate without involvement of the principal broker.

Security Deposits

An important, although sometimes confusing, aspect of property management is the interaction of the license law and the Uniform Residential Landlord and Tenant Act, Chapter 383 of the Kentucky Revised Statutes. This Act applies to residential rental property in those cities, counties, and urban-county governments that adopt the provisions of the Act. The Act has not been adopted in most of Kentucky, but, according to 201 KAR 11:245, Section 1(2)(i), licensees are required to comply with KRS 383.580 (the statute that regulates security deposits).

Section 1 of KRS 383.580 (Uniform Residential Landlord and Tenant Act) requires landlords to keep tenant's security deposits in an account in a bank, or other lending institution, regulated by Kentucky or the federal government. The account must be used only for the purpose of holding security deposits, and the tenant must be given the name of the institution holding the funds as well as the account number. Although KRS 324.111(7) that allows property management funds to be held in the principal broker's escrow account (either the broker's general escrow account or an account set up specifically for property management), that does not include security deposits as required under KRS 383.580(1) which requires a separate account for security deposits.

Under Section 2 of the Uniform Residential Landlord and Tenant Act, the tenant must be given a list of existing damage to the property prior to occupancy and must be given the opportunity to view the property to ascertain the accuracy of the list. Both the landlord and the tenant must sign the list to show they agree to the damages listed. If, however, the tenant does not agree with the list, he must give the landlord a written and signed statement specifically listing the disputed items. This list is referred to as the initial damage listing.

When the tenant vacates the premises, Section 3 of the Uniform Residential Landlord and Tenant Act requires the landlord to inspect the premises and compile a list of damages that were not on the initial list. That list must be provided to the tenant with an estimated cost for repairing the damage that contains an indication of the amount that will be withheld from the security deposit. The tenant shall have an opportunity to either agree with the list or disagree with it. If he agrees with the list, he signs. However, if he disputes items on the list, he must state his disagreement in writing and affix his signature. This list is referred to as the final damage listing.

a notice to attend a KREC proceeding is not an invitation, but a demand. KREC subpoenas may be enforced by the circuit court if someone fails to comply.

Verified Complaint: The document filed with the Kentucky Real Estate Commission when someone wants to complain about the actions of a real estate licensee. Verification means that the complaint must be signed and notarized. Forms may be found on the KREC website: www.krec.ky.gov.

Kentucky Real Estate Commission

Real estate agents in Kentucky must be licensed by the Commonwealth of Kentucky to practice real estate brokerage. The **Kentucky Real Estate Commission**, often referred to by the acronym KREC, or simply as the Commission, has, in the past, had complete authority to administer the licensing process for those obtaining and holding a real estate associate or brokers license. On December 1, 2016, all of that changed. The Governor signed an Executive Order making major changes in the way the KREC operates and how it fits in into the government hierarchy. Those changes are included in this section. As of the writing of this book the changes seem to relate mainly to the administration of the KREC and not to day-to-day activities of the licensees. That being said, because the law is new, and as all new laws are, open to interpretation and challenge, licensees are encouraged to obtain legal advice for themselves if they have a legal matter that may be affected by these changes.

License laws can be found in KRS 324 and KRS324B, and the Kentucky Administrative Regulations in 201 KAR 11. Licensees are encouraged to watch the KREC website and newsletter for updated information.

The new hierarchy is the **Public Protection Cabinet** at the top with a Secretary, then the **Department of Professional Licensing** with a Commissioner, the **Kentucky Real Estate Authority** with an Executive Director, and the Kentucky Real Estate Commission with the day-to-day operations handled by an **Administrative Coordinator** who also handles the Board of Home Inspectors.

One thing that did not change is the underlying purpose of the KREC to protect the interests of the public who are dealing with real estate licenses. Regulating licensees includes both conducting licensing examinations for people desiring a real estate license and disciplining licensees who violate the license laws or regulations after they are licensed. KRS 324.281. As part of the discipline process, the KREC is authorized to investigate alleged violations by licensees and to hold hearings to determine whether or not violations occurred. If it is determined that a violation did, in fact, occur, the Commission has the power to discipline the licensee. Additional duties include promulgating regulations with the approval of the executive director of the Kentucky

Real Estate Authority. Another function of the KREC is to participate with other agencies for the improvement of the administration of statutes and regulations. KRS 324.281(5).

In addition to its duties of licensing and regulating licensees, the KREC is also charged with conducting educational seminars and courses for continuing education within the field of real estate. As part of the educational process, the Commission requires all licensees licensed after June 19, 1976 to take mandatory education classes. KRS 324.281(7). The KREC must also create a process for developing continuing education classes, including the approval of schools and instructors. KRS 324.281(8).

The Kentucky Real Estate Commission is located at 10200 Linn Station Road, Louisville, KY 40223. In the past, the KREC staff have been available by phone at (502) 425-4273 or (888)373-3300, by fax at (502) 426-2717, or e-mail at www.krec.ky.gov, to answer questions from licensees and consumers. At the time of writing this book, the KREC Commissioners have approved the legal staff's request that they respond only to license law and regulation questions presented by principal brokers. Associates are encouraged to discuss any question they may have with their principal broker. If the principal broker does not know the answer, she can contact the KREC legal staff for the answer. These questions must be related to the license law and regulation, not personal legal issues relating to specific real estate transactions. It is easy to see how much time responding to individual licensees would involve. There has been no change in responding to questions from consumers.

One of the major changes is the creation of the Kentucky Real Estate Authority (a/k/a Authority and KREA) within the Department of Professional Licensing. KRS 324B.050. This entity oversees the Kentucky Real Estate Commission, the Board of Real Estate Appraisers, the Board of Auctioneers, and the Board of Home Inspections. The four entities have one Executive Director who is appointed by the secretary of the Public Protection Cabinet with prior written approval from the Governor.

The Authority has taken over many of the tasks that have, in the past, been conducted by the Kentucky Real Estate Commissioners. KRS 324B.050(3) sets out its power and authority. Services provided by the Authority to each of the four boards include handling personnel staffing and administrative support; establishing and maintaining office space as well as supplies and furniture needs; publicizing the Authority, while making information available to the public; employing an administrative coordinator for each of that boards to carry out the administrative functions and day-to-day operations of the particular board; and entering into agreements as necessary for the Authority and boards.

For these services, the Authority may charge the KREC and other boards a reasonable amount for its services and those of its employees. Neither the executive director of the Authority, or the administrator coordinators for the boards, are classified employees.

Expenses and Fees of the Commission

All fees and charges paid by licensees to the Commission, except those paid for the real estate education, research, and recovery fund, shall be deposited into the general fund of the state treasury. Amounts paid by the licensees for the real estate education, research, and recovery fund are addressed in KRS 324.400.

Expenses incurred to operate the KREC are paid from the general fund of the state treasury. The expenses of the Commission shall not exceed the total amount collected for fees, charges, fines, and penalties outlined in KRS 324.286.

Fees charged to licensees by the Commission for various services are outlined in KRS 324.287. Because most of the fees are stated as fees "not to exceed" a set amount, the licensee must consult the KREC to determine the exact amount for each fee. This information can also be found on the KREC website at www.krec.ky.gov.

Examination fees for taking the sales associate and broker licensing exams cannot exceed one hundred dollars ($100). The original license fees for both brokers and sales associates cannot exceed thirty dollars ($30.00). Broker's and sales associate's license renewal fees cannot exceed thirty dollars ($30.00). When a licensee wants to transfer from one **principal broker** to another principal broker, the fee charged by the KREC cannot exceed ten dollars ($10.00). A request for any change by a licensee to the KREC cannot exceed ten dollars ($10.00). A licensee's annual payment to the **real estate education**, research, and recovery fund cannot exceed thirty dollars ($30.00), and is paid the first time at the time of the original licensing, and then at the time of license renewal. When an applicant for a broker or sales associate license applies for a criminal records check, the fee cannot exceed thirty dollars ($30.00). KRS 324.287.

When a licensee needs a certification of license status, the fee is ten dollars ($10.00). KRS 324.330(3); KRS 324.287. This certification states whether or not the licensee is in good standing with the KREC. A licensee may need such a certification when applying for another state issued license, such as, an insurance sales person's license, a license to practice law, or a securities' license. An application for a real estate sales license in another state may require a certification from Kentucky.

Commissioners

Commissioner Appointments

The Kentucky Real Estate Commission has five Commissioners that are appointed by the Governor for a three-year term. Four of the Commissioners must be licensees who have been active in real estate for at least ten years and who have resided in the state for at least ten years. One of the commissioners must be a citizen at large who is neither associated with, nor has a financial interest in, the practice or business of real estate. KRS 324.281(1). No more than three Commissioners can be from the same political party and there can only be one Commissioner from any given county. KRS 324.281(4). Commissioners may serve no more than two consecutive terms. KRS 324.281(2).

Commissioners are compensated at the rate of three hundred dollars ($300.00) per day for official business subject to an annual maximum of six thousand dollars ($6,000.00). They will be reimbursed for all expenses paid and incurred in the discharge of official business consistent with the reimbursement policy for state employees. The executive director of the Authority must approve travel for Commissioners and staff. KRS 324.281(9). At this point, nine monthly meetings are held each year (check KREC website for dates) by the Commissioners to consider KREC business, including licensee discipline, educational programs, changes in the real estate industry, and the general business affairs of the KREC. These meetings are open to the public and licensees may attend to keep abreast of the current activities of the Commission.

At the time of the Governor's Executive Order, three of the current Commissioners were changed to ex-officio members. Under that order, these three members would serve out their current terms; however, they would not be voting Commissioners. The new KRS 324B does not address the ex-officio position; therefore, it is unclear if that position will continue or be dissolved.

Commissioner appointments are made by the Governor from a list provided by the **Kentucky Association of REALTORS®.** The Kentucky Association of REALTORS® is the trade association that real estate licensees may join. If a licensee chooses to become a member of the trade association, he is referred to by the trademark designation: **REALTOR®.** KAR is an acronym often used for the Kentucky Association of REALTORS®, and it also refers to the Kentucky Administrative Regulations (the licensing regulations). All REALTORS® are licensees, but not all licensees are REALTORS®. The Kentucky Real Estate Commission and the Kentucky Association of REALTORS® are separate organizations independent of each other. Occasionally, the KREC and KAR work together on projects that will benefit both the consumer and the licensees.

The appointee list presented by the Association to the governor must have at least three (3) names for each vacancy, and there is no requirement that licensees on the list belong to the Association. However, as a practical matter, generally, the four licensed Commissioners are, in fact, REALTORS®. Once the KAR list is submitted to the Governor if he does not wish to choose one from that list, he may request another list. Should a vacancy occur during the year, the Governor fills the vacancy from the names remaining on the list for that year or, at his discretion, obtains a new list from the Association. An appointment made for an unexpired term shall be for the remainder of that unexpired term. KRS 324.281(3).

****

Case: Challenging Constitutionality of KRS 324.281(3)

Kentucky Ass'n of Realtors, Inc. v. Musselman, Ky., 817 S.W.2d 213 (1991)

This case was filed as a declaratory judgment action by Chester W. Musselman, a licensed real estate agent, who was not a member of the Kentucky Association of REALTORS®, and who felt that it was unconstitutional under the Kentucky constitution to require Governor Wallace Wilkinson to appoint a commissioner from the list prepared by the Kentucky Association of REALTORS® A declaratory judgment action is one that is filed to ask the Court to rule on a matter of law when the party wants to determine his legal rights.   In addition to the Association, the Kentucky Real Estate Commission, the Governor of Kentucky, and the Attorney General of Kentucky were named as parties to the action.

Mr. Musselman's lawsuit, filed in Jefferson Circuit Court, alleged that, because only about one-third of the approximately 24,000 real estate licensees were members of the Kentucky Association of REALTORS®, KRS 324.281, Section (3), was unconstitutional. He felt that the statute is arbitrary and in violation of Section 2 of the Kentucky Constitution, that it violated the separation of powers principle in Sections 27 and 28 of the Kentucky Constitution, and also infringed on Section 69 that vests "supreme executive power of the Commonwealth" to the Governor.   The Jefferson Circuit Judge agreed with Mr. Musselman, and the case was appealed to the Court of Appeals by the Association and the Attorney General.   Because of the potential impact on other statewide administrative agencies, the Court of Appeals recommended that the case be transferred to the Kentucky Supreme Court.   The Supreme Court agreed to accept the case.

At page 214 of the decision, the Supreme Court reasoned:

> "The statute limits the power of the Governor to appoint two names on a list provided by the Association, but it neither limits appointees to   members of the Association nor does it compel the Governor to appoint someone on the list. Strictly speaking, the Association may nominate any licensed real estate agent who meets the qualifications in Subsection (1) of KRS 324.281, without regard to membership in the Association, and the Governor may reject all the names on the list provided by the Association and forego making an appointment until provided with a list that includes a person whom the Governor deems suitable for appointment to the office."

The Court went on to say that the KREC has the power to designate the qualifications and other criteria for service as commissioners, as long as the qualifications and criteria are not impermissibly "arbitrary" within the context of the Kentucky constitution.   The represented by legal counsel. If the complainant chooses not to retain legal counsel, the general counsel of the KREC will help the complainant present the complainant's evidence. Although the complainant is getting assistance from the Commission's general counsel, the general counsel is not representing the complainant; rather, she is prosecuting the case for the KREC.

Opening remarks are made by the hearing officer about the process that will be followed and any specific rules the hearing officer wants to be followed. Once those remarks are completed, the parties are each given an opportunity to make an opening statement. An opening statement simply sets forth the party's version of the facts, the evidence that will be produced, and the inferences that may be drawn from the evidence.

After the opening statements are completed, the complainant presents his evidence. When each of the complainant's witnesses finishes his testimony, the respondent has a right to cross-examine the witness. Once all of the complainant's evidence has been presented, the respondent presents her evidence. Respondent's witnesses may be cross-examined by the complainant. During the evidence presentation, the hearing officer rules on the admissibility of evidence and other objections that may be raised by either party, as well as asking questions of the witness.

At the conclusion of the presentation of the evidence, the parties may make closing arguments. Closing arguments review the facts and evidence that was presented, and encourage the hearing officer to believe the version of the facts and evidence as presented by the party making the closing argument. If requested by the parties, the hearing officer may agree that the closing arguments be submitted in writing. This gives the parties a chance not only to review the facts and evidence presented, but also gives them a chance to brief issues of law that may have arisen during the hearing.

The hearing officer will submit to the commissioners a document entitled "Findings of Fact and Conclusions of Law." Recommended sanctions may also be included in his report. Basically, the hearing officer sets out what she believes the facts to be based on the evidence presented, and how the law would be applied based on those facts. At this point, the parties may present to the KREC a document taking exception to the facts and conclusions as determined by the hearing officer.

When the case is placed on the agenda of a monthly KREC meeting, the commissioners consider the case based on the information presented to them from the hearing officer in the "Findings of Fact and Conclusions of Law." The commissioners may agree with the hearing officer's findings and conclusions, or they may reject, amend, or remand the case. After they make their decision, the Kentucky Real Estate Authority Executive Director will review their decision and issue the final order. See KRS 324.200(2).

Appeal If either or both parties disagree with the KREC decision, an appeal may be taken to the Circuit Court in the county where the respondent has her principal place of business. KRS 324.200(2). When the appeal is taken, the KREC and the Executive Director, is his capacity as Executive Director for the Kentucky Real Estate Authority, are two of the appellees (parties defending the appeal). As an appellee the KREC must convince the Circuit Court that its decision on the case was appropriate, considering the evidence presented at the hearing. Additional evidence cannot be presented by either party to the Circuit Court, because the Circuit Court is acting as an appeals court and not as a trial court. At its discretion, the Circuit Court may ask the parties to participate in an oral argument, or they may choose to review the written briefs of the parties and the evidence in the file.

Discipline is automatically stayed (held in abeyance, stopped) during the pendency of the appeal unless the final order states otherwise. KRS 324.200(3)

Once the Court of Appeals has rendered its opinion, either party may ask the Supreme Court of Kentucky to review the case. Review by the Supreme Court is totally at the Court's discretion. If the Supreme Court chooses not to review the case, the decision of the Court of Appeals is final. Of course, if the Supreme Court agrees to review the case, it can only consider briefs of counsel and evidence presented at the hearing before the Kentucky Real Estate Commission. Unless a party has an issue that may be considered by the federal courts, and most real estate cases do not include such issues, the decision of the Kentucky Supreme Court is final.

The discussion in this chapter relating to hearings before the KREC has centered on licensees who have had complaints filed against them. However, the same rules apply if the KREC refuses to issue an applicant a license for any reason. The license applicant may request a hearing before the Commission to argue that a license should be issued.

****

Kentucky Real Estate Commission Quasi-Judicial Authority Case

McAlister & Co. v. Jenkins, 214 Ky. 802, 284 S.W. 88 (1926)

This case began when certain individuals (names not provided in the case) filed a complaint with the real estate commission alleging that McAlister had obtained a listing on their property through his salesmen. According to the complaint filed with the commission, the listing was obtained through misrepresentation and improper practices by McAlister's salesmen. Affidavits supporting the allegations against McAlister and his salesmen were filed with the real estate commission.

A hearing was held and the evidence presented convinced the three presiding real estate commissioners that McAlister's salesmen had violated the law. Based on the improper conduct of the salesmen, their licenses were revoked. McAlister was, however, found not guilty of the charges.

Although he was not found guilty of the violation, the commissioner's order stated:

"While the commission is unable from the evidence submitted to find G. H. McAlister guilty of violation of any of the provisions in clause 8 of the real estate license law, yet it feels that he is morally responsible for the acts of his salesmen in selling real estate, and while he testified that he did not know of the transactions between the complainants and his salesmen, E. I. Rawles, yet we consider it was his duty as the head of the firm to know, and he should know the method employed by his salesmen in selling and listing property through his office."

McAlister felt that these statements were falsely and maliciously made by the commissioners to damage McAlister although he was not found guilty of the charges. In addition to publishing the statements in the commission order, the statement was contained in reports to the newspapers for publication.

A lawsuit against Jenkins and the other two commissioners was filed in the Jefferson Circuit Court alleging that the statement was false and without foundation, that it was defamatory to his business, and that the commissioners conspired to injure his business. The Jefferson Circuit Court agreed with Mr. Jenkins and the other commissioners that the statement was absolutely privileged. Mr. McAlister appealed the decision to the Kentucky Court of Appeals.

In deciding the case on appeal, the Court looked to the licensing statutes and the requirements under those statutes that were imposed on the real estate commission. The Court determined that the licensing regulations required the real estate commission to act in a quasi-judicial capacity in regulating the activity of licensees. Under the statute, the commissioners had the duty to investigate allegations of wrongdoing by licensees, hold hearings, and penalize agents found to have violated the laws.

The language of the Court at page 807 states:

> "So we have imposed upon the member of this commission by express provisions of law, the duty to hear complaints, the duty to fix the time of hearing, and the duty to notify in writing the person or persons whose rights may be affected by the hearing. We have imposed upon them the duty to conduct such a hearing and to hear the evidence adduced by either party, and finally to determine after hearing such evidence what the rights of the parties are with respect to the subject matter involved, and we have a solemn legislative declaration that their findings upon such hearing shall be conclusive."

Because of the clear provisions of the statute, the Court found that the commissioners clearly had legislative authority to hold the hearing and to render an opinion. And, as

125

agents of the state in the exercise of their duties they were participating in quasi-judicial functions. While they were acting on behalf of the state in a quasi-judicial capacity they had an **absolute privilege** to make the statement about Mr. McAlister. An absolute privilege gives the judicial officer protection, when acting in his judicial capacity, from lawsuits for slander, libel and defamation.

The Court reasoned:

> "If in the discharge of a duty imposed by law a public official clothed with quasi-judicial powers may have suspended over his head continually the threat of libel suits, it is apparent that his official conduct would be tempered by and tainted with the fear that he might be unjustly subjected to such actions. The policy of the law…the rule is, that although upon rare occasions judges…may maliciously slander…in the exercise of their authority, it is better that they should be protected….It is a rule …not designed to protect the malicious official…to protect the whole public from weak and vacillating public service by those upon whom such duties are imposed.

Although the court was not absolutely certain that the comments in the order were necessary to determine the guilt of the salesmen, they served as an admonition to Mr. Alistair that he should be more careful and more businesslike in running his business. The court also felt that the statement was probably designed to have an effect on others engaged in the real estate business.

****

Since this case was decided in 1926, and is still relevant today, it is clear that the Kentucky Real Estate Commission is considered by the courts to be a quasi-judicial body. As such, it has the authority to hold hearings and discipline licensees within the parameters set forth in the statutes without fear of a libel action by the licensee disciplined.

Limitation on Jurisdiction

Over the years there has been continuing debate of whether or not the KREC has jurisdiction over homeowner's associations, neighborhood association, condominium and townhouse associations, not for-profit community associations, and other business activities that involved real estate, but that was not directly the brokerage of real estate. KRS 324.2812 was passed a few years ago to state that the authority of the Kentucky Real Estate Commission does not extend to these groups.

Summary

The Kentucky Real Estate Commission is the administrative agency that regulates real estate licensees. Although the primary purpose of the Commission is to protect the interests of the public by licensing, educating, and regulating real estate agents, the Commission staff is available to assist licensees when they have questions and concerns regarding the license law.

The new hierarchy is the Public Protection Cabinet at the top with a Secretary, then the Department of Professional Licensing with a Commissioner, the Kentucky Real Estate Authority with an Executive Director, and the Kentucky Real Estate Commission with the day-to-day operations handled by an Administrative Coordinator who also handles the Board of Home Inspectors. The Commissioners no longer manage the business affairs of the commission. That is handled by the Executive Director of the Kentucky Real Estate Authority.

Commissioners are appointed by the Governor from lists that are provided by the Kentucky Association of REALTORS®. The commissioners serve for three year terms and are paid $300.00 per meeting with a maximum payment of $6,000. Four of the commissioners are real estate licensees and one is a consumer member without financial interests in the real estate industry. Commissioners, like licensees, are held to high ethical standards. A commissioner may be removed from office for committing a felony crime with fraud as one of the elements, for moral turpitude, missing meetings, being negligent, and not following a code of ethics.

Fees collected by the KREC from the licensees for various services, as well as fines that are assessed as discipline, are deposited into the state treasury. Expenses to operate the Commission are paid from the state treasury and the budget cannot exceed the fees deposited.

The real estate education, research, and recovery fund is a fund established and managed by the KREC. In addition to paying damages to consumers damaged by licensees who commit fraud, the fund also pays for real estate education for both licensees and consumers, as well as funding research to improve the real estate industry.

Anyone believing a licensee has violated the licensing law may file a verified complaint with the KREC. The KREC may, on its own motion, file a complaint against a licensee. Once the complaint is filed, if its sets forth a prima facie case, the licensee is required to answer the complaint, and it will also be investigated. After the investigation is completed, the complaint will be dismissed if the investigation reveals that a prima case has not been established by the complainant, or will be set for a hearing if the investigation determines that the license laws or regulations may have been violated. This hearing is referred to as a formal hearing.

Prior to the formal hearing, the KREC usually schedules a pre-hearing. A pre-hearing gives the parties an opportunity to settle the case without a formal hearing. The pre-hearing is voluntary and, in the event, either party refuses to attend, the matter proceeds to the formal hearing.

If the commissioners decide to have a formal hearing, both the complainant and the respondent will have the opportunity to present evidence. The hearing will be conducted either by a quorum of the commissioners or a hearing officer from the Public Protection Cabinet. After the hearing, the hearing officer will file "Findings of Fact and Conclusions of Law" with the commissioners who will review the information, make their decision, and forward to the Executive Director of the Kentucky Real Estate Authority for his review and for issuance of the Final Order.

Once the Final Order is entered, rendering an opinion on the case, either party has a right to appeal the decision to the Circuit Court in the county where the licensee does business. When the appeal is filed in the Circuit Court, the KREC must be named as one of the appellees. The Circuit Court must consider the appeal based on the record in the case, and not on new evidence. After the Circuit Court decision, the parties may appeal that decision to the Court of Appeals. At the conclusion of that appeal, the parties may ask the Supreme Court of Kentucky to consider the case. If the Supreme Court refuses to hear the case, the decision of the Court of Appeals is final.

KRS 324.2812 limits the KREC jurisdiction, stating specifically that the KREC jurisdiction does not extend to community association managers and the management or business activities of not for-profit community associations, which includes townhouse, condominium, homeowner, and neighborhood associations.

CHAPTER 5

LICENSE LAW VIOLATIONS
Improper Conduct, Prohibited Practices, Sanctions

Statutes and Administrative Regulations

Chapter Objectives

This chapter reviews various ways in which a principal broker or sales associate may violate the licensing laws. In addition to violations, this chapter includes sections on improper conduct and prohibited practices by licensees, as well as the discipline that may be imposed against licensees by the Kentucky Real Estate Commission. Frequently asked questions that will be answered in Chapter 5 are:

1. Does the license law state specific license law violations?
2. Can a principal broker be punished if an affiliated licensee violates the law?
3. Does a violation of the fair housing laws also violate the license laws?
4. What is a net listing?
5. What activities by licensees constitute improper conduct?
6. What practices by licensees and non-licensees are prohibited under the license law?
7. Can the Kentucky Real Estate Commission discipline agents who violate the law?
8. If so, what are the sanctions the KREC can impose against a licensee?
9. Does the Commission have jurisdiction over unlicensed individuals?
10. If the KREC finds someone practicing without a license, what process must it follow?
11. Will a licensee lose his license if he is arrested for committing a felony?
12. May a licensee personally buy real estate without notifying the seller as long as he pays full listing price?
13. Can a licensee have a license law violation that leads to a criminal penalty?
14. May a principal broker guarantee a seller that the property will sell in a certain amount of time for a certain price?
15. Can a principal broker offer a buyer a $1,000 for buying property from one of the principal broker's associates?

The KREC allows licensees to speak with sellers who have their property listed with another principal broker about listing their property at the expiration of the current listing if, and only if, the seller calls the licensee. If the listed seller calls a licensee about listing the property when the current listing expires, the licensee should have a form signed by the seller stating that it was the seller who called the licensee and not the licensee who called the seller.

In July 2009 the KREC legal counsel developed the form to be used. Unfortunately, most licensees do not know the form exists. It may be found on the KREC web site and is entitled: "Seller-Initiated Re-listing Request Disclosure Form". One of the problems with licensees finding the form is its title. This is not a re-listing -- it is a new listing by a new broker. The form needs a new title.

Not only can the licensee, if called by the seller, talk about listing the property, the licensee may actually list the property with a beginning date beginning when the current listing expires. A licensee discussing a listing with a currently listed seller should take care not to say anything that would lead the seller to believe the licensee is encouraging her to terminate the current listing.

(p) *"Publishing or circulating an unjustified or unwarranted threat of legal proceedings or other action."* Licensees may not threaten buyers, sellers, landlords, tenants, and other licensees with unjustified or unwarranted legal action. This subsection specifically says "unjustified or unwarranted threats" of legal action; however, the best practice for licensees is not to threaten anyone with legal action. If be believes legal action is warranted, he should consult an attorney and follow the attorney's advice.

(q) *"Failing or refusing on demand to furnish copies of a document pertaining to a transaction dealing with real estate to a person whose signature is affixed to the document."* When a party to a real estate transaction signs a document, she is entitled to a copy at the time of signing. 201 KAR 11:090. Not only is it a violation of the license law to fail to provide the document at the time of signing, this subsection makes it a violation for the agent to fail, or refuse, to deliver a copy when it is requested. This subsection addresses parties who actually sign the document requested. Licensees should remember that their files are confidential and information from their files should not be released to anyone, unless the person requesting the information has legal authority to have the information. Remember, that something as simple as a phone number, the seller's new address, or who attended the closing, is confidential information. If a person has signed a form, she may have a copy of it as long as her signature is on it. Otherwise, licensees should not release documents without a subpoena. And, of course the KREC has the authority to ask to see the file.

(r) *"Failing, within a reasonable time, to provide information requested by the commission as a result of a formal or informal complaint to the commission which may indicate a violation of this chapter."* The Kentucky Real Estate Commission clearly has authority to investigate licensee activities that may violate the license law. As part of its authority to investigate, the KREC has the authority to request copies of documents as a

result of a complaint. A licensee who fails to cooperate and produce the documents within a reasonable time will be in violation of this subsection. "Reasonable" has not been defined in the statutes and regulations; however, because the KREC controls the license, it would be wise of the licensee to cooperate and produce the requested information in a timely manner. Licensees have the right to consult legal counsel if they are contacted by the KREC about a possible license law violation. Depending on the situation, the E&O insurance carrier may pay for legal counsel. Errors & Omissions policies vary, but this is an avenue that may be available to the licensee. A prudent licensee should follow-up with legal counsel *before* producing requested information and participating in an interview with an investigator.

(s) *"Paying valuable consideration to any person for the name of potential sellers or buyers, except as otherwise provided in KRS 324.020(4)."* Only licensees may be compensated for real estate brokerage activities. Referring buyers and sellers to a broker or sales associate involves the practice of real estate and that requires a license. If a broker or sales associate pays an unlicensed person for names of potential buyers and sellers, she is in violation of this subsection. Principal brokers should always verify that anyone asking for a referral fee has an active real estate license. The license does not have to be a Kentucky license.

(t) *"Violating any of the provisions in this chapter or any lawful order, rule, or administrative regulation made or issued under the provisions of this chapter."* This is an "add-on" section. A licensee violating any of the licensing statutes, administrative agencies, or orders of the Kentucky Real Estate Commission or Court, would be liable for that violation as well as for a violation of this section.

(u) *"Any other conduct that constitutes improper, fraudulent, or dishonest dealing."* This subsection gives the Commission the opportunity to review the facts of a specific situation to determine if the licensee acted improperly, fraudulently, or dishonestly. Specific instances of **improper conduct** are set forth in 201 KAR 11:121 and in KRS 324.160(5). Fraudulent dealing is defined in 201 KAR 11:011(4), as making a material **misrepresentation** that is known to be false, or made recklessly, that induces a person to act in reliance on the statement which causes damage. Dishonest conduct is not specifically defined in the licensing regulations, but the KREC could make this determination based on generally accepted standards of honesty. In the event the facts reveal improper, fraudulent, or dishonest dealings, this subsection would be included in the charges against the licensee.

(v) *"Gross negligence."* **Gross negligence** is a term used most often in criminal cases, personal injury cases, and accident cases to indicate that someone acted recklessly and with indifference to the safety of others. Although it has not been defined in Kentucky case law relative to real estate licensees, by reading other types of cases it appears that an agent may be found liable for gross negligence if he fails to use common sense and reasonable skill that other licensees would use in similar situations. Although the term is difficult to define, cases have often used terms like "failure to use slight care" and "failed miserably in performing tasks" when reaching the conclusion of gross negligence.

The only instance of a violation rising to the level of "gross negligence" is a violation of 201 KAR 11:045, Sections 1 and 2. This section of the licensing regulations relate to the minimum standards that must be met by licensees representing sellers and buyers.

KRS 324.160(5)

"Any conduct constituting an act of discrimination regarding a person's race, color, creed, sex, or national origin, including use of scare tactics or blockbusting, shall be considered improper conduct as referred to in subsection (4)(u) of this section." This section of the license law makes it clear that licensees may not discriminate in their real estate business. Protected classes under the fair housing laws include race, color, creed (religion), sex, national origin, familial status, and handicap. Some areas of Kentucky include "sexual orientation" as a protected class. The National Association of REALTORS® has added "gender identity" as a protected class in its Code of Ethics. Although not specifically included in the list of protected classes under the license law, it is likely the KREC would consider discrimination based on "sexual orientation" or "gender identity" to be improper conduct. The licensee best standard of practice is to treat everyone they work with the same.

KRS 324.160(6)

*"No unlawful act or violation of any provision of this chapter by any affiliated licensee shall be cause for holding the principal broker primarily liable, unless the broker has knowledge of the unlawful violation and did not prevent it. The principal broker and his or her designated manager, if any, shall exercise **adequate supervision** over the activities of licensed affiliates and all company employees to ensure that violations of this chapter do not occur. The failure of a broker or his designated manager to exercise adequate supervision of the licensed affiliates shall constitute a violation of this chapter."* Principal brokers and their designated managers who are aware of unlawful activity by brokers and sales associates affiliated with the office and fail to prevent it may be held primarily liable for the violation. If a principal broker or designated manager becomes aware that a licensee is breaking the law, he must take steps to stop it, or he will be primarily liable, along with the licensee. For example, a principal broker who knowingly allows his agent to materially misrepresent the condition of a certain piece of property would be primarily liable to a violation of this statute. Instead of being liable simply for failing to adequately supervise the licensee, he would also be liable for the misrepresentation.

Principal brokers and their designated managers must adequately supervise their affiliated licensees. "Adequate supervision" is a term that is difficult to define. What may be adequate supervision for experienced brokers and sales associates may not be adequate for new licensees. That standard requires that principal brokers have policies and practices in place so that the licensees know the law, know what is expected of them in the performance of their duties, and know that the principal broker expects them to adhere to all laws, policies, and procedures. The principal broker, or someone designated by her, should be available to answer questions and to assist the agents when they need help. Failure to adequately supervise is a violation of the license law and may result in penalties separate and apart from the penalties imposed on the licensee for a license law violation.

KRS 324.160(7)

"The practice of obtaining, negotiating, or attempting to negotiate net listings shall be considered improper dealing." Because of the possibility of a licensee taking advantage of an uninformed property seller or buyer, net listings are illegal in Kentucky and most other states. A net listing is a listing in which the seller agrees to accept a base sales price and the agent may have all money received over that price. An example would be a seller who wants $100,000 for his property and agrees with the agent that the commission will be for all money received over $100,000. If the property sells for $101,000 the agent receives $1,000; however, if it sells for $150,000 the commission received by the agent is $50,000. All compensation for brokerage services must be specifically stated as a percentage of the sales price, a flat fee, or other named compensation. Although not seen often, the compensation may be something other than money (for example, a car).

Improper Conduct

The administrative regulations in 201 KAR 11:121 sets forth specific actions by licensees that are improper. In addition to this regulation, actions that are considered "improper conduct" are found in other regulations. A licensee found to have acted improperly may be disciplined by the KREC under KRS 324.160(4)(u).

Referral Fees

It is improper for a licensee to accept or agree to accept a referral fee from any person in return for directing a client or customer to that person for goods, services, insurance, or financing, unless written notice is given. The written notice must be given to the buyer and seller if the transaction is for the purchase and sale of real estate, and given to the lessor and lessee if the transaction is for a lease. This provision does not affect the practice of paying referral fees between licensed brokers when one broker refers a client or customer to another licensed broker for real estate services. 201 KAR 11:121, Section 2(1).

Although this provision permits acceptance of referral fees, as long as written notice is given to the parties, licensees must be aware of the federal Real Estate Settlement Procedures Act. RESPA, as the law is commonly referred to, prohibits referral fees or kickbacks in the delivery of settlement services. Included in settlement services are services provided by the lender, attorney, settlement agent, appraiser, inspector, surveyor, real estate agent, insurance agent, and credit reporting agencies. Acceptance of referral fees from any of these people may be a violation of RESPA and subject the licensee to penalties federal and state penalties as well as KREC sanctions.

Refusal to Show Property

Refusing to show prospective purchasers listed property, or in any way prohibiting them from viewing the property, is improper conduct, unless the seller has given the licensee a specific written and signed directive. 201 KAR 11:121, Section 2(1)(b). Licensees must carefully review the seller's request to make sure the seller is not discriminating against prospective purchasers. Sellers and licensees may not discriminate against members of the **protected classes**, which, as previously stated, include the following: race, color, religion, national origin, sex, familial status, or handicap. In addition to these protected classes, parts of Kentucky have added "sexual orientation" as a protected class in housing, and the NAR Code of Ethics has added both "sexual orientation" and "gender identify."

Although it is improper conduct to refuse to show prospective purchasers listed property, it is not improper conduct to refuse to allow another licensee to show the property. This regulation does not make it mandatory for the listing agent to cooperate with other agents. When considering agency relationships and fiduciary duties owed to clients, it is not in the client-seller's best interest for the listing agent to refuse to cooperate with other licensees because the more agents trying to sell the property the more likely it is to sell. Having the property sold is in the best interest of the seller. Although not required by law, a principal broker who refuses to cooperate with selling agents would be prudent to obtain the written consent from his sellers.

This section does not require the listing licensee to compensate a cooperating licensee who shows and sells the property. If the listing licensee allows a cooperating agent to show the property, the agents should discuss and agree prior to the showing if compensation will be paid to the cooperating company and, if so, how much. The cooperating agent would be wise to get the agreement with the listing broker in writing. Because of the statute of frauds, the cooperating principal broker could not enforce his right to a commission without a written, signed agreement.

Fiduciary Duties

This regulation lists the **fiduciary duties** owed a client by the licensee. These are the same fiduciary duties that have always been recognized in common law. It is improper conduct for the licensee to fail to follow any of these fiduciary duties when representing a client.

Fiduciary duties are: loyalty, obedience to follow lawful instructions, disclosure, confidentiality, reasonable care and diligence, and accounting. 201 KAR 11:121, Section 2(c)). The duty of loyalty means that the licensee must be faithful to the client's best interest in representing him in the purchase, sale, or lease of real property. A licensee must promote the client's interest above everyone else's interest, including his own.

Licensees must obey the lawful instructions of their clients. Although the licensee must follow legal instructions, licensees should review all instructions to make sure they are legal. A client's instruction to violate disclosure or fair housing laws should not be followed. It is not a defense for the licensee who violates the law to say that his client instructed him to do so.

Clients are entitled to full disclosure by the licensee. Licensees should disclose to their clients all material information relating to the property, to the contract, to relationships between the parties, and everything else that arises during the transaction. Material information is information that, if known by the client, would make a difference in decisions made by the client during the transaction. Whether or not the roof leaks would be material information needed by the client when making an offer. For the seller client, it would be material to know whether or not the buyer had to sell another piece of property before closing. For both the buyer and seller it would be "material" to know that the agent is related to one of the parties.

Licensees must keep client information confidential. Although licensees should never discuss their client's business with anyone else, the licensing law defines confidential information as: "information that would materially compromise the negotiating position of a party or prospective party to a real estate transaction if disclosed to the other party." 201 KAR 11:400. The duty of confidentiality extends beyond the representation. After the agency relationship ends, the licensee must continue to keep the client's information confidential forever. Confidentiality is the one fiduciary duty that does not terminate with the agency relationship.

Agents owe their clients the duty of reasonable care and diligence. While representing the client, the licensee must exercise the amount of care and diligence that is generally recognized in the industry as acceptable representation. The agent should use as much skill and diligence in handling the transaction as any other agent. This is generally referred to as "meeting the standard of care in the industry." Failure to exercise reasonable care and diligence is not only a breach of fiduciary duty, but may also be considered negligence or gross negligence. Negligence and gross negligence can result in license law sanctions as well as other legal sanctions, including lawsuits.

A breach of the duty of accounting is probably the easiest kind of fiduciary breach to prove when alleged. Licensees owe their clients an accounting of all money collected and spent on the client's behalf. Accounting issues arise when a licensee fails to deposit earnest money or releases it without proper authority. Property management disputes also frequently raise the accounting issue when a licensee collects rent and pays for repairs without forwarding complete information to the owner of the property. Because of the paper trail left by checks, bank statements, and receipts, accounting cases are usually resolved by a review of the documentation. This is the fiduciary duty that can lead to criminal indictments when breached.

Guaranteed Sales Plans

A guaranteed sales plan is defined in two different ways. One, is as an offer or solicitation to guarantee the sale of an owner's real property. The other is to guarantee the purchase of the owner's real estate if the owner's real is not sold by the broker while it is listed. 201 KAR 11:121.

Section 2(1)(d) sets out in detail how the guaranteed sales plan must be advertised. The advertisements must state whether or not a fee will be charged, whether or not the real estate must meet certain qualifications, whether the purchase price to be paid by the licensee be determined by the licensee or a third party, and whether or not the owner will be required to purchase other real estate through the licensee. This subsection also details the size of print in the advertisement. Verbal advertisements must meet certain clarity standards. Licensees should consult this section in the license law manual to assure compliance in advertising.

Violation of Statute or Administrative Regulation

The last subsection of 201 KAR 11:121, Section 2, holds licensees liable for improper conduct for violating any of the licensing statutes or administrative regulations that govern brokers, sales associates, or real estate transactions. This is clearly a "catch-all" and "add-on" for charges against licensees.

Fees and Other Compensation

It is not clear why this subsection appears in this part of the license law; however, it does. 201 KAR 11:121, Section 2(2) states that it is not improper to advertise the fee or other compensation the licensed agent agrees to charge for his services. Agents sometimes question advertisements that contain competitors' commissions thinking that such advertisements may be anti-trust violations. According to the KREC legal counsel, these ads are fine.

Prohibited Practices

KRS 324.165 outlines another practice considered "improper conduct." In the last few years, with the increase in national relocation services and national referral networks, licensees have seen an increase in the number of demands for referral fees from people and companies that have not, to the knowledge of the licensee, been involved in the real estate transaction. This situation may arise when an employer contracts with a relocation company to assist their employees who are being transferred into and out of Kentucky.

Agents that have worked with either a buyer or seller that is being transferred often receive a demand, sometimes weeks after the closing, for a referral fee for the transaction. KRS 324.165 prohibits this practice. Nothing in this statute prohibits licensees from entering into referral fee arrangements with referring agents and relocation companies.

Section (1) has two provisions. First, no person shall solicit or request a referral fee unless the referring person introduced the business to the licensee and the referring person and licensee enter into a contract for the referral fee. This section requires a prior contact to enter into an agreement before the fee is requested and allows the licensee to accept the referral.

The second provision in this section prohibits any person from threatening to reduce or withhold employee relocation benefits, and prohibits taking action that is adverse to the interests of the licensee's clients. This provision is intended to assure the employee that, because his real estate agent does not agree to pay the referral fee to the relocation company, he will not be penalized by his company and lose relocation benefits. Obviously, this statute tries to control the actions of local, state, national, and international companies. Whether or not the statute will be effective will be determined in the future after cases proceed through the courts.

Another aspect of this statute deals with people who may counsel buyers and sellers, who already have a real estate agent, to terminate those relationships to enter into new ones with licensees approved by the relocation and referring companies. This provision is designed to prevent one licensee from interfering with another licensee's listing contact, buyer agency contract, or other agency agreement.

This statute does not prohibit companies from communicating relocation policies and benefits to their employees, as long as the communication does not advise or encourage the employee to amend or terminate an existing contract between the employee and his agent. To advise or recommend that the employee amend or terminate a current agency relationship is clearly a **prohibited practice** under this statute.

Section 3 of KRS 324.165 states that a licensee violating this statute shall be engaging in improper conduct as set forth in KRS 324.160(4)(u.) It further states that a violation by an unlicensed person would subject that person to penalties under KRS 324.990. The KREC may sanction a licensee for a violation because of its control over licensees, but it is unlikely that an unlicensed person would be prosecuted for this behavior.

SANCTIONS

The KREC may impose sanctions on licensees after a formal hearing. There are seven possible penalties, and those are set out in KRS 324.160(1). These are also the sanctions that may be offered a licensee to settle a complaint without a hearing.

Revoking the licensee's license is obviously the most serious penalty. KRS 324.010(18) defines revocation as: "the status of a license when disciplinary action has been ordered that removes the licensee's legal authority to broker real estate for a minimum of five years."

Once the agent's license is revoked, he cannot apply for a new license for five years from the date of revocation. At the end of the five year period, the licensee may apply for another license, but whether or not another license will be issued is completely at the discretion of the KREC. If the Commission decides that he may have another license, he must take the examination and meet all educational requirements in effect at the time. KRS 324.220. The Commission, in deciding whether or not a new license may be issued, considers the nature of the violation that led to the revocation and the likelihood of the licensee violating the license law again.

After a hearing, if the KREC decides the licensee should not practice real estate for a period of time, it may suspend the license for this period. Suspension under KRS 324.010(17) is defined as: "the status of a licensee when disciplinary action has been ordered against a licensee that prohibits the brokerage of real estate for a specific period of time." At the end of the suspension, the licensee may again practice real estate. Although the licensee may not work in real estate and earn commissions during the suspension, commissions that have been earned prior to the suspension may be paid to the licensee. KRS 324.160(3).

In addition to the violations set forth in KRS 324.160 that may lead to the suspension of an agent's license, failure to complete continuing education requirements and failure to repay damages that have been paid from the real estate education, research, and recovery fund, will also lead to a suspension of the license. Failure to repay damages to the recovery fund may also lead to revocation of the license at the discretion of the KREC.

The licenses of brokers and sales associates affiliated with a principal broker who has had his license suspended or revoked will automatically have an inactive status until they affiliate with a new principal broker. Once they re-affiliate with another principal broker, their licenses will be issued at no cost if they re-affiliate in the current license year. KRS 324.230. If they do not transfer to a new broker until the next license year, they will have to pay the license renewal fee due that year.

If the Commissioners decide the violation was not serious enough to either suspend or revoke the license, it may place the licensee on probation for a period of up to twelve (12) months. The KREC may place restrictions on the licensee during the probation period. Two examples of restrictions are: requiring the licensee to meet with the Commission investigator periodically to review brokerage practices; and, requiring the licensee to provide certain documentation to the KREC at set intervals. If there are further violations during the probationary period, the licensee may be sanctioned for the new violation and may have additional penalties imposed for the first violation.

Broker: A person who holds a broker's license issued pursuant to KRS 324.046. A broker may or may not also be the Principal Broker of the real estate company that holds her license.

Broker-affiliated training program: One or more post-license educational courses offered for post-licensed education credit provided or sponsored by a real estate principal broker.

Broker Core Class: In recent years, the Kentucky Real Estate Commission created a new core class that was open only to licensees with a broker's license. The class was titled "Risk Management for Brokers." This class could be taken by qualified licensees instead of the Kentucky Core class. Material in the class is more advanced and in greater detail than the material in the Kentucky Core class. In December 2015, after the course material was revised, the Commissioners voted to allow not only licensees with a broker's license to take the class, but also associates who are designated managers, office managers, team leaders, and any other licensee in a management position. Each attendee with an associate's license must submit an affidavit, satisfactory to the KREC, stating that she is, in fact, in a management position.

Broker Management Class a/k/a Broker Management Skills Class: This is a class approved by the KREC that all applicants for the broker's license must take and complete prior to taking the broker's licensing examination. Providers submit outlines and course materials for the KREC approval. 201 KAR 11:450.

Business Relationship: This term is used in conjunction with Parts 1 and 2 of the Agency Disclosure form required by the KREC. When completing either Part 1 or Part 2 of the form, the licensee must indicate if an ongoing business relationship with another party to the transaction exists and/or if he has ever been involved in a prior real estate transaction with another party to the transaction.

Buyer Agency: The agency relationship existing between the licensee and the buyer where the licensee represents the buyer and no one else in the transaction. In this relationship, the licensee owes fiduciary duties only to the buyer.

Client: The party in an agency relationship who is represented by the agent. May also be referred to as the principal.

Commercial Property: This phrase is commonly used to refer to non-residential income producing properties, although it may be applied to apartment complexes. For licensee purposes, commercial property is defined in 201 KAR 11:400 as property other than a single-family residential lot or dwelling, agricultural property, or multi-family property containing less than four units.

Commercial Real Estate Brokerage: As used in KRS 324.235 - KRS 324.238, any parcel of real estate located in this state that is lawfully used for sales, retail, wholesale, office, research, institutional, warehouse, manufacturing, or industrial purposes; lawfully used primarily for multi-family residential purposes involving five (5) or more dwelling units; or zoned for a business or commercial use by a planning unit pursuant to KRS Chapter 100.

Commingling: The process of depositing client funds into the brokerage's account or into the broker's personal account.

Commissioner (KRS 324B) and Commissioners (KRS 324): When Commissioner is used in reference to KRS 324B, the word means the Commissioner of the Department of Professional Licensing. When Commissioner or Commissioners is used in reference to KRS 324, the word refers to the five people appointed by the governor to provide services as outlined in KRS 324(5) to the Kentucky Real Estate Commission. Licensees will most often use the word when they are talking about the five commissioners at the Kentucky Real Estate Commission not the one Commissioner at the Department of Professional Licensing. However, close attention must be paid to the context of the statement being made now that two statutes relating to the KREC use the same term for two different positions.

Complainant: The person who files a complaint with the Kentucky Real Estate Commission against a licensee who is referred to as the respondent. In most legal matters, the complainant is referred to as the plaintiff.

Confidential Information: As used in the licensing law, any information that would materially compromise the negotiating position of either party to the transaction.

Consent to Service: Out-of-state principal brokers sign a "consent to service of jurisdiction" document agreeing that they may be sued in Kentucky. Otherwise, a consumer wanting to file a lawsuit against the principal broker would be required to file the lawsuit in the state where the principal broker does business and/or resides (depending on that state's laws). Filing a lawsuit outside of Kentucky against a principal broker for negligence in Kentucky would create a hardship on the consumer. Signing this form is one of the KREC requirements for allowing an out-of-state principal broker to do business in Kentucky.

Contact: When used in the licensing law, a discussion or correspondence between a licensee and another person relating to the licensee's brokerage services.

Continuing Education: Education relating to the practice of real estate and real estate law that must be taken annually by licensees, unless they were licensed prior to June 19, 1976, or after January 1, 2016. Licensees licensed before June 19, 1976 are not required to take Continuing Education classes. And, licensees licensed after January 1, 2016 do not have to take continuing education for the first two years of licensure, because they are taking post-license classes. After the two-year post licensing classes, these licenses are on the regular continuing education schedule. The KREC must approve the course content and instructors. KRS 324.085 and 201 KAR 11:230.

Continuing Education Providers: Effective December 4, 2015, 201 KAR 11:230, was created to address all continuing education provider requirements for classes and related issues. Approved Real Estate Schools that offer continuing education classes are also referred to as Continuing Education Providers.

Cooperating Broker: When the listing principal broker permits another principal broker to sell or lease her listed property, the principal broker bringing the buyer or tenant to the transaction is known as the cooperating broker or "co-op." The cooperating broker has no contractual relationship with the seller or owner of the property and is paid his/her commission by the listing broker. On occasion, the co-op is paid by his buyer client.

Counteroffer: When an offer is made by the offeror that is not acceptable to the offeree, the offeree may reject that offer and make an offer back to the offeror known as a counteroffer. Any change made to the original offer is a counteroffer.

Criminal Records Background Check: Applicants for a license must obtain a criminal records check from the FBI or from any other commission-approved criminal background-checking provider or company furnishing identification records that are comparable to those provided by the FBI, as determined by the commission. At this time, the applicant may use the Kentucky State Police Process to request their FBI report. The background check must be ordered prior to taking the examination. 201 KAR 11:430.

Customer: In real estate transactions, the person who is not represented by an agent is known as the customer.

Deceptive Advertising: Under the license law, advertising that is untrue, and the licensee placing the ad knows that it is not true.

Delinquency Plan: A licensee who does not complete his continuing education classes by December 31st may enter into a plan with the KREC to complete the classes. 201 KAR 11:230, Section 6.

Delivery: This term has several different meanings in real estate law. The term may be used to indicate that a written document has actually been delivered to a person as required by the licensing laws. Examples of delivery include delivering the sellers disclosure of property condition (KRS 324.360), delivering the agency disclosure form (KRS 201 KAR 11:400), and the delivery of all forms signed by a party in a real estate transaction (201 KAR 11:090). Actual delivery of documents in other real property contexts require that certain documents be delivered from one party to the other to consummate the transaction. These situations require the grantor to deliver the deed to the grantee to convey title and the mortgagor to deliver the mortgage to the mortgagee to convey a lien interest.

Department of Professional Licensing a/k/a Department: This is a Department in the Public Protection Cabinet that provides administrative services, technical assistance, and advice to several boards and commissions including the Kentucky Real Estate

Commission. KRS 324B.030. The Commission shall be appointed by the Governor. KRS 324B.020.

Designated Agency*:* Under the license law, a principal broker, in an in-house sale, may appoint one agent to represent the seller and one agent to represent the buyer. The licensing statute sets forth specific instructions on how the designation must occur, and it requires the principal broker to remain a limited dual agent, representing both the seller and buyer.

Designated Manager: A licensed sales associate or broker who manages a main or branch office for the principal broker, at the principal broker's direction, and has managing authority over the activities of the sales associates at that office. KRS 324.010(11).

Discovery*:* In a judicial setting, including a KREC case, the process of learning the facts and evidence that the other parties in the case intend to use at the trial. Discovery may be taken by oral evidence in a deposition or by written testimony in affidavits and interrogatories.

Dual Agent*:* A licensee who is representing both the seller and buyer, or the landlord and tenant, in the same transaction. *Another definition:* In a real estate transaction in which the principal broker and all of her agents represents both the seller and the buyer.

Due Process: A person's constitutional right to be present at the hearing, to present evidence, and to have the case decided based on a set of rules and principles that apply equally to all parties.

Duty of Accounting*:* The fiduciary duty of the agent to inform the principal about all monies received and disbursed by the agent on behalf of the principal.

Duty of Confidentiality*:* The fiduciary duty of the agent to keep all of the principal's personal information confidential. These confidences must be kept not only during the representation, but they must be kept secret forever.

Duty of Disclosure*:* The fiduciary duty of the agent to inform the principal about all material facts surrounding the property and the transaction. This duty extends not only to the physical condition of the real property, but also to any fact that would affect the principal's decisions regarding the purchase or sale of the property.

Duty of Loyalty*:* The fiduciary duty of the agent to protect the interests of the principal above the interests of all others, including those of the agent.

Duty of Obedience to Lawful Instructions*:* The fiduciary duty of the agent to follow all legal instructions of the principal even if the agent does not agree with the instructions.

Duty of Reasonable Care and Diligence: The fiduciary duty of the agent to use at least the same level of skill and effort in representing the principal as another agent would use.

Earnest Money: Money given to the seller by the buyer that shows the buyer is acting in good faith and that the buyer intends to perform the contract. Funds are generally held by the real estate broker in her escrow account as stated in the sales contract. There is common misconception that real estate sales contracts cannot be created without earnest money. That is not correct, in that the contact must have consideration, but not necessarily earnest money.

Earnest Money Deposit: When a buyer enters into a sales contract to purchase property, the buyer generally gives the seller a deposit to show he is acting in good faith. This money is referred to as the earnest money or a good faith deposit. In transactions involving real estate brokers, this deposit is generally held in the broker's escrow account; however, the parties may agree that the deposit will be delivered directly to the seller.

Errors and Omissions Insurance: Professional liability insurance (commonly referred to as E&O Insurance) that must be carried by all active licensees. KRS 324.395. Licensees whose licenses are in escrow are not required to carry E&O Insurance. KRS 324.310(2).

Escalation Clause: A clause in the offer that automatically increases the purchase price in the offer in an amount specified in the event the seller receives another higher offer before the offer with the escalation clause expires.

Escrow Account: The account that must be maintained by principal brokers to hold all money coming into the brokerage belonging to someone else. Earnest money deposits and property management funds are the two most common reason for holding money in the escrow account. KRS 324.111 regulates these accounts.

Executive Director: This person manages the Kentucky Real Estate Authority. He is appointed by the Secretary of the Public Protection Cabinet with prior written approval from the Governor. KRS 324B.050. The duties of the Executive Director are outlined in KRS 324B.060.

Executory Contract: A contract that is in the process of being performed by the parties. Once the contract closes, it becomes known as an executed contract.

Express Agency: An expressed agreement, either oral or written, in which the principal and agent agree to create an agency relationship. This is the opposite of an implied agency which is created by the actions of the principal or agent.

False Advertising: Under the licensing law, advertising that is contrary to fact. Simply stated, untrue information. 201 KAR 11:011(3).

INDEX

CASE LAW

Regulations